EXECUTIVE COACHING for RESULTS

EXECUTIVE COACHING *for* RESULTS

THE DEFINITIVE GUIDE
to
DEVELOPING ORGANIZATIONAL
LEADERS

Brian O. Underhill, Kimcee McAnally, John J. Koriath

Foreword by
Marshall Goldsmith

Afterword by
Richard Leider

BERRETT-KOEHLER PUBLISHERS, INC.
San Francisco

Berrett-Koehler Publishers, Inc., 235 Montgomery Street, Suite 650, San Francisco, CA 94104-2916, Tel: (415) 288-0260 Fax: (415) 362-2512 www.bkconnection.com

Ordering Information
Quantity sales. Special discounts are available on quantity purchases by corporations, associations, and others. For details, contact the "Special Sales Department" at the Berrett-Koehler address above.
Individual sales. Berrett-Koehler publications are available through most bookstores. They can also be ordered directly from Berrett-Koehler: Tel: (800) 929-2929 Fax: (802) 864-7626 www.bkconnection.com.
Orders for college textbook/course adoption use. Please contact Berrett-Koehler: Tel: (800) 929-2929 Fax: (802) 864-7626.
Orders by U.S. trade bookstores and wholesalers. Please contact Ingram Publisher Services, Tel: (800) 509-4887 Fax: (800) 838-1149 E-mail: customer.service@ingrampublisherservices .com or visit www.ingrampublisherservices.com/Ordering for details about electronic ordering.

Berrett-Koehler and the BK logo are registered trademarks of Berrett-Koehler Publishers, Inc.

Printed in the United States of America

Berrett-Koehler books are printed on long-lasting acid-free paper. When it is available, we choose paper that has been manufactured by environmentally responsible processes. These may include using trees grown in sustainable forests, incorporating recycled paper, minimizing chlorine in bleaching, or recycling the energy produced at the paper mill.

Library of Congress Cataloging-in-Publication Data
Underhill, Brian O., 1969–
Executive coaching for results: the definitive guide to developing organizational leaders / Brian O. Underhill, Kimcee McAnally, John J. Koriath; foreword by Marshall Goldsmith; afterword by Richard Leider.
p. cm.
ISBN 978-1-57675-448-1 (hardcover : alk. paper)
1. Executive coaching. 2. Executive ability. 3. Leadership. I. McAnally, Kimcee, 1957– II. — Koriath, John J., 1953– III. Title.
HD30.4.U53 2008
658.4'07124--dc22   2007029212

First Edition
17 16 15 14 13   10 9 8 7 6 5 4 3 2

Contents

Figures and Tables

Foreword

Marshall Goldsmith

In many ways executive coaching is still a primitive and newly emerging field. Both leaders and companies are struggling with, "Exactly what does an executive coach do?" and "What can executive coaching do for our company?"

Although quite a few books have been written on coaching at a micro or individual level, few have addressed coaching at a macro or organizational level. Many books have discussed how an individual can be a great coach for one leader, yet little has been written on how organizations can create great coaching processes that impact many of their leaders. *Executive Coaching for Results* presents the first truly comprehensive look at how major organizations can and should use executive coaching to develop their leaders.

Executive coaching is a next evolutionary step in the development of leaders. Historically, leadership development was largely focused on participants' involvement in training programs. These programs were all based upon one completely invalid assumption—if they *understand*, they will *do*.

Wrong!

As I write this foreword, my newest book, *What Got You Here Won't Get You There*, is listed in the *New York Times* as the #4 best-selling "advice" book in the United States. The #1 best seller is (of course) a *diet* book. Even though my book sold more copies than any other business book in America last week, the top-selling diet book sold *ten times* as many copies! Everyone who buys diet books makes the same assumption as everyone who goes to training programs: If I *understand* how to go on a *diet*, I will do it.

Wrong again!

As the sales of diet books have skyrocketed in the United States, readers have become more and more obese! You don't lose weight by reading diet books. You lose weight by actually going on a diet—and sticking with it.

My partner, Howard Morgan, and I conducted extensive research involving more than 86,000 participants in leadership development programs from eight major corporations.[1] Our findings are hard to dispute. If leaders attend training programs, but then don't discuss what they learn with co-workers and follow up to ensure continued progress—they improve no more than by random chance. In other words, they might just as well have been watching sitcoms all day!

Over the years I have learned that many participants in training programs actually do apply what they have learned, and they do get better. Many don't! Why do so many leaders attend training programs, return to work with a short-term "religious conversion experience," and then end up making no real change? The answer is seldom because of a lack of values or a lack of intelligence. Almost all of the participants in the training programs that I have conducted over the years are both very good people and very smart people.

The reason why many leaders don't apply what they learn in traditional training when they're "back on the job" is that they are buried in work. Leaders in major corporations today work harder than leaders have worked in the past 40 years. They feel trapped in an endless sea of e-mails, voice mails, and requests. They worry about global competition. The job security that they may have felt in the past is a distant memory. They barely have time to meet the minimum requirements of their jobs—much less focus on their long-term development as leaders.

Executive coaches can help leaders bridge the huge gap between understanding what to do and actually *doing it*. Your coach is a person who sticks with you over time and makes sure that you do what you know you should do, but have a tendency to "put off until tomorrow"—a tomorrow that (without help) may never come.

Even though many major business publications have recognized me as a expert in the field of coaching, I still have my own coach—Jim Moore. I have been asked, "Why do you have a coach? Don't you understand the theory of how to achieve positive change in behavior?"

I *wrote* the theory! That's why I have a coach. I know how hard it is to achieve positive, lasting change. I am no better than the people I work with; I am just as busy, just as over-committed, and just as crazy. If I didn't have a coach to give me ongoing advice, support, and encouragement, I would tend to slip back, just like anyone else.

One of my good clients is a highly respected CEO of a major corporation. I had completed a very successful coaching assignment with one of his top executives and he asked me to work with another top leader. I asked him, "Why do you want me to do this? You understand my coaching process as well as I do. You have been to my class three times. Why don't you do this coaching yourself?"

His candid response helped explain why he is a great CEO. He replied, "There are four reasons that I want you to take this coaching assignment instead of me: (1) I don't like dealing with behavioral issues, so my motivation is very low; (2) Although I understand the theory of what you do, you have far more experience at it than me—so my ability is not that great; (3) I have absolutely no time; (4) Your fees are high, but your time is worth a lot less than mine!"

I thought about his response and realized that he was exactly right. If I were that CEO, I would hire an executive coach to develop my top talent—in the same way that he was hiring me!

My CEO friend helped me understand why executive coaching is here to stay. In today's corporate world, the stakes have gone up, the pressure has gone up, and the need to develop great leaders has gone up. The time available for executives to do this has diminished. Coaching can help high-potential leaders become great leaders!

Looking ahead to the future, executive coaching will continue to increase in importance. Organizations will need to learn how to manage coaches and the coaching process. As this need becomes greater, the learnings in *Executive Coaching for Results* become more important.

As you read this book, think about your own organization. Learn from the great examples. And to paraphrase a hero of mine, Buddha, *use what works for you and let go of the rest!*

Preface

The journey for this book has been the result of a series of events during the past four years. Like many works before ours, it was simply a story whose time had come.

The Background

In 2004, Executive Development Associates (EDA) conducted its bi-annual survey of *Trends in Executive Development*.[2] More than 100 Fortune 1000 and Global 500 companies responded.

The findings identified executive coaching as the fifth most prevalent learning method among 25 possibilities (Table 1). More importantly, executive coaching represented a top-five learning method for the first time since the study's inception in 1984. Fifty-six percent of corporations said that they used external executive coaching as a learning methodology (Fig. 1).

Concurrently, EDA observed a marked increase in coaching-related queries from executive and leadership development practitioners affiliated with its networks. A poll of EDA's network members in 2005 verified that 64 percent of respondents felt that an industry study would be *very* or *extremely valuable* for them.

Table 1   Top Five Learning Methods (2000 vs. 2004)

2000	2004
Action Learning	Senior executives as faculty
Outside experts	Action Learning
Senior executives as faculty	Outside speakers
Outside speakers	Outside experts
Inside experts	**External executive coaches**

Figure 1.   Top ten learning methods (2004) (select all that apply).

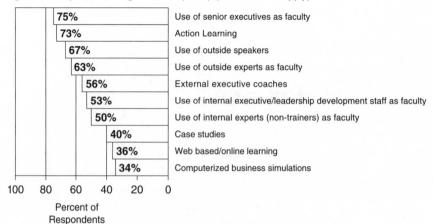

75%	Use of senior executives as faculty
73%	Action Learning
67%	Use of outside speakers
63%	Use of outside experts as faculty
56%	External executive coaches
53%	Use of internal executive/leadership development staff as faculty
50%	Use of internal experts (non-trainers) as faculty
40%	Case studies
36%	Web based/online learning
34%	Computerized business simulations

100   80   60   40   20   0

Percent of
Respondents

As a result, we worked with EDA—along with the guidance of an exemplary advisory board—to conduct the *High Impact Executive Coaching*[3] research study in the spring of 2005.

The Research

High-Impact Executive Coaching would be the first research to examine the industry from a *three-dimensional* perspective: learning from organizations, leaders being coached, and executive coaches (Fig. 2).

We used a rich mixture of qualitative and quantitative data collection methods. Forty-five in-depth interviews were conducted across the three perspectives (19 organizations, 13 leaders, 13 executive coaches). A Web-based survey achieved breadth, having been completed by 48 organizations, 86 leaders (from 25 companies), and 152 coaches. Please note that the surveys were open to all leaders and coaches, but a leader and his or

Figure 2.   Three-dimensional high-impact executive coaching methodology.

Organization
Perspective

Leader   Executive Coach
Perspective   Perspective

her specific coach did not necessarily answer the same survey. In addition, in-depth case studies explored practices at Fidelity, General Mills, IBM, and Intel.

The Beginnings

Although the data was valuable, the conversation it catalyzed was invaluable. The *High Impact Executive Coaching* data was presented in July 2005 during a two-and-a-half-day Study Workshop that brought together nearly 25 senior practitioners to examine and interpret study findings, as well as to advance the state of the art in the industry. The group shared a phenomenal energy, in which the work of coaching was seen in a framework of developing authentic leaders across the workforce and embedding values in organizational culture that would enable companies to thrive in the 21st-century paradigm of global, interconnected teams and networked talent. In such a framework, coaching is charged with providing development for leaders that hones business acumen and nurtures emotional and social intelligence, for the full engagement that today's complex business challenges require.

Coaching owners were assembled from some of the world's top companies—Intel, TimeWarner, Unilever, IBM, BP, Sony, Wal-Mart, and many more. Sitting in front of us were reams of slide decks—data from the first *three-dimensional* (organizations, coaches, leaders) research study on executive coaching.

Our job for the next three days was to make sense of the findings, share company best (and worst) practices, and come to conclusions that we believed would shape this industry for years to come.

In her opening remarks at the conference, Mary Jane Knudson, vice president for human resources at Fidelity Investments, described the psyche of organizations overall as being characterized by a "persistent and pervasive sense that we are in over our heads." This remark and the imagery it suggests made a lasting impression on many as we tried to consider just what we'd gotten ourselves into.

Imagine the power: a consortium of influential companies raising the state of the art in the coaching business!

The research and that summit were the beginnings of the book you now hold.

The Book

Building on the groundbreaking work in the EDA research study and in Minneapolis, this book—*Executive Coaching for Results*—rapidly advances the industry. It uses a combination of the original research, the authors' experience, and first-hand learnings from some of the world's finest organizations.

This book brings together these voices by sharing practical learning, best practices, and experiences that demonstrate the collective intelligence of the field.

It will be the first to gauge the executive coaching business in the corporate world, featuring the research and best practices from many name-brand organizations.

Although the research and practitioners assembled to create this book are often from large corporations, the thinking, insights, and practices discussed here have valuable application in any size business. If an organization has a need to link the efforts of its talent to business strategy; if it has a culture whose values, competencies, and capabilities shape performance; and if it recognizes that sometimes even the small changes made in the behavior, style, and relationships of a key leader can serve as a tipping point for bottlenecked energy in an organization—then the perspectives in this book will prove valuable.

Our Introduction begins by explaining why this book is important now, how the industry has grown, and why we believe coaching has now come of age.

Chapter 1 offers definitions and the purpose of coaching, along with a description of who receives coaching today. Chapter 2 examines the importance of organizational culture and leadership support for a company's program. In Chapter 3 we illustrate the link of coaching to leadership development strategy, talent management, and human resource practices. We also explore the role of internal professionals in coaching assignments.

Chapter 4 provides details for coaching engagements, including activities during coaching engagements, assignment lengths, how coaches and leaders interact, and the costs of coaching. Chapter 5 walks us through common instruments used in a coaching assignment, explains how assessments are used, and offers suggestions about what should be in a coach's toolbox. In Chapter 6 we examine the debate about what level of consistency companies should have across coaching assignments.

Chapter 7 explores the increasing use of internal coaches, the benefits and challenges internal coaches face, and how internal and external coaching compare. Chapter 8 addresses the debate on measuring the impact of coaching, and what methods and metrics can be used. In Chapter 9 we discuss the art of finding, locating, and screening qualified coaches; whether coaches should be certified; and the importance of matching leaders and coaches.

Chapter 10 is about designing a world-class coaching community. We offer practical recommendations and solutions to assist leaders in maximizing their coaching experience and explain how the pool can be a resource for the organization. This chapter also includes examples of what some companies are doing to stay connected to coaches. Chapter 11 explores life after coaching—what happens when assignments end, and the types of on-going arrangements.

And finally, Chapter 12 highlights the newer forms of coaching, summarizes industry trends, and forecasts the future of the coaching industry.

Throughout the chapters, company practitioners share highlights of their coaching programs. These indented articles (*callouts*) are generally three to four paragraphs long and explain the company's practices.

Note: The data from the interviews for the research depended on a high level of confidentiality. Therefore, all quotations from organizations, coaches, and leaders are anonymous in order to protect the privacy of the individuals who shared their experiences with us.

The Journey

A few words of explanation are in order as you begin this journey. Throughout the book, we use the terms *executive coaching* and *coaching* interchangeably. Unless otherwise stated, references to *research* refer to the *High Impact Executive Coaching* research study. To clarify another point, this book is about *executive* coaching—not to be confused with *life* coaching, which seeks to help people achieve personal goals. There is a confusing divide between these disciplines within the industry; but they have different coaches, practices, and qualification standards. This is a book on executive coaching.

We invite you to join your colleagues on this journey. Join with us to continue this conversation, explore case studies, read best practices from leading organizations, and advance the coaching cause. This content will continue to live and grow at www.executivecoaching4results.com.

Acknowledgments

This book has become a reality as a result of countless conversations and discussions with family, colleagues, and friends. As most authors know, although their name is on the front cover, the effort of writing a book involves collaboration with many, many, *many* people.

We'd like to start by acknowledging the people and companies who provided the original inspiration for the book, the original research study. Thanks to Mike Dulworth and James F. Bolt from Executive Development Associates, who sponsored the research; and co-researchers Sue Brown, Carol Braddick, and Kerry O'Hara, who did a fabulous job in bringing the research to life.

A very special thanks to all the practitioners and companies who participated in the original research or shared their best practices for the book—Agilent Technologies; Alcan; Bell Canada Enterprises; BP; California Public Employees' Retirement System; Credit Suisse; Dell, Inc.; Fidelity Investments; General Mills; IBM; Intel Corporation; Johnson & Johnson; McDonald's; NCR Corporation; Progressive Group of Insurance Companies; Saudi Aramco; Sony Corporation; The Conference Board; The Walt Disney Company; Thrivent Financial for Lutherans; UBS; Unilever; Wal-Mart; and Xerox. These companies have generously donated their time and information to advance the knowledge on coaching.

And special thanks also to Kimberly Arnold, Carol Braddick, Sue Brown, Mary Wayne Bush, Kim Deustch, Susan Diamond, Margaret L. Durr, Harris Ginsberg, Heidi M. Glickman, Bob Gregory, William Hodgetts, Alison Hu, Sam Humphrey, Barbara Kenny, Anthony I. Lamera, Christine Landon, Dorothy Lingren,

Janet Matts, Mary O'Hara, Kristin Olsen, Kenneth J. Rediker, Elaine Roberts, Pat Santillanes, Stephen E. Sass, Lori Severson, Deborah Swanson, Zepnep Tozum, Janet Weakland, and Kevin Wilde for their insights and contributions throughout the book.

We'd like to express our gratitude to Marshall Goldsmith and Richard Leider for writing the Foreword and Afterword and for their support of this project. In addition, thank you to Larry Lyons for his encouragement from the beginning of this process.

We greatly appreciate the encouragement of our supporters at Berrett-Koehler—most notably Johanna Vondeling, who has from the beginning provided amazing guidance and enthusiasm for the project; Jeevan Sivasubramaniam, whose continual efforts enabled the book to stay on track, coordinated, and on time; and to Steven Piersanti, for publishing our book and bringing together an amazing team at BK who truly make it a pleasure to collaborate with as authors. We also appreciate the efforts of the reviewers and copyeditors who provided feedback and shared their insights on our original manuscript: Philip Hamer, Philip Heller, Lori Long, Regina Sacha, Leigh Wilkinson, and Susie Yates.

Brian would like to give a heartfelt thank you to my beautiful bride Lisa, daughter Kaitlyn, and son Evan. I'd also like to thank my parents Robert and Aysegul, my brother Stephen, and Natalie Dodd. Thank you for believing in this project since the start and in this profession for much longer. And thank you to all the clients, coaches, and colleagues who have been great supporters over the years.

Kimcee would like to acknowledge the many friends who have been supportive throughout this process. In particular, thanks to Danny, Glenn, Greg, Janel, Janet, Joe, Julie, Karen, Ken, Kevin, Lori, Martin, Meredith, Pam, Sue, and Steve for your enthusiasm to get me through the process! Thanks for your understanding and listening to tales about the book adventures. And much appreciation to my business partners, colleagues, and clients who have been supportive as I've juggled time for the book and work this past year.

John would like to express his appreciation to Kathryn, Alexandra, and the community that enliven their daily life. Also many thanks to the EDA team that supported this project and the network of practitioners, leaders, and coaches who inspire the human spirit.

Introduction

Coaching Has Come of Age

Coaching has now come of age.

Given the rapid and extensive growth of this industry, it is not surprising that there is confusion regarding the field of executive coaching among corporations, coaches, and the executives who seek a coach. There currently is no *official* voice of the corporate coaching industry. Thus there is a clear, unfilled need among corporate coaching practitioners for a definitive source on corporate coaching.

Organizations worldwide are scrambling to make the most of this highly touted, yet somewhat mysterious, development intervention. What is coaching? What happens in coaching? How do you find good coaches? How do you know whether coaching has been successful?

Why Now?

Just within the past ten years the coaching industry has realized explosive growth. There are now an estimated 40,000 coaches worldwide,[1] with an estimated $1–2 billion in yearly revenues. Many organizations are now making external coaching a high priority in their leader development strategies. Some are now five to ten years into an in-depth coaching implementation, serving hundreds—if not thousands—of their executives. Coaching has achieved a place as both a professional and a profitable business.

A 2004 Harvard Business Review article[2] coined the industry the *Wild West* of coaching, in response to the prevailing mood of the time. Major organizations sponsored several industry-wide research studies to get a better handle on this promising methodology.

What explains this incredible growth? For one thing, the ever-increasing pace of change requires organizational leaders to develop quickly, and in the context of their current jobs. Traditional training programs are often set up to train or educate large numbers of people, but not to focus on a specific individual's development needs. Coaching offers an individualized development option without removing leaders from their work.

Second, the war continues for leadership talent. As the hunt to find and retain talent intensifies, many companies have viewed coaching as a way to compete in the marketplace to attract and retain that talent. Several organizational leaders we met said they would not still be at their companies if they hadn't received coaching.

Coaching in organizations grew with the rise of 360-degree feedback deployment in the early 1990s. Companies began offering one- or two-hour debrief sessions with an external coach to review the feedback. Organizations found that the feedback seemed to *stick* better, and leaders liked the opportunity to work with an unbiased external professional. More leaders, as well as many intact teams, found the process helpful for their development—and as leaders grew as executives, they recommended coaching to others.

Gradually, the standard coaching offer expanded to several sessions, several months, and eventually to 6- to 12-month assignments, and beyond. Coaches were a mixture of consultants and trainers, psychologists, and former leaders inside industry. Organizations began to target coaching for high-potential or high-performing leaders, rather than those experiencing performance problems.

Today, name-brand organizations such as Dell, Johnson & Johnson, Wal-Mart, and Unilever have large managed coaching programs serving countless executives and use pools of highly-screened coaches, in all parts of the world. Coach qualifications are now more consistently understood, and coaches operate in more countries than ever before. In addition to individual coaches, organized coaching networks, boutique firms, and large players serve the industry.

Coaching is also moving internally, with many organizations training internal practitioners to coach leaders. This idea is popular primarily for expense purposes and with companies who view their organizational culture as highly unique. Internal coaching is most frequently being implemented at the mid-manager and first-line supervisor level. External coaches remain the most popular solution for executives.

Coaching's rise in popularity impacts the use of traditional executive development methods. We found that in-house training, formal mentoring, and external education are at times being displaced by executive coaching. As a result, many trainers and consultants now deliver their specialized content with coaching included. For example, a time management class may now include follow-on coaching sessions.

We are also seeing more organizations looking to create a *coaching culture*. Companies are training their leaders to better coach others in work-related situations. As more organizations understand the results of coaching, they are offering *leader-as-coach* training.

The benefits include one-on-one focused development, specialized personal learning, confidentiality, and personal accountability for improvement. In addition, coaching provides leaders the opportunity to develop individual capabilities faster than most instructional programs can, and in areas where training programs do not exist. The main challenges for coaching remain its relatively high costs and difficulty in measuring results.

Generally, senior leadership's support and enthusiasm for coaching is on the increase. This can easily vary from company to company, however. We also found a gap between leaders receiving coaching and those willing to publicly endorse coaching to others. Perhaps there is still a stigma attached to having a coach in some companies.

Although coaching is still a rapidly growing field, many answers and best practices are now available to guide the development of the industry. The industry is not as out of control as some would suggest. The Wild West is being tamed (as it was in real life).

The industry's growth is showing no signs of slowing down. A recent Hay Group survey[3] of HR professionals found that more than 50 percent had established a coaching program in the past 18 months. Coaching was estimated to be growing at about 40 percent per year. Another survey by The Chartered Institute of Personnel and Development[4] found that 79 percent of responding companies were using coaching.

In the following review of coaching, The Conference Board shares trends from its industry-leading conferences.

Conference Trends in Executive Coaching

Susan Diamond
The Conference Board

Executive coaching has become an accepted best practice in the field of executive and management development, evidenced by the fact that two conferences and two seminars staged by The Conference Board are dedicated exclusively to the topic of executive coaching.

Begun in the early 2000's, the first coaching conferences attracted audiences seeking basic knowledge about an emerging field, which commonly focused on executives who needed *fixing*. As coaching evolved from a remedial intervention into a perk for C-suite and high-potential executives, knowledge and sophistication about coaching practices have increased. In response, The Conference Board added seminars and forums in 2004 to satisfy the interests of more senior-level practitioners.

Corporate presenters, Advisory Board members, and attendees at these events engage in active dialogue. They represent such leading public, private, and government institutions as Morgan Stanley, Colgate Palmolive, Bank of America, Dell, Prudential, Getty Images, Pfizer, Prudential, 20th Century Fox, Johnson & Johnson, H. O. Penn Caterpillar, McGraw Hill, McKinsey, Pepsi Cola Bottling Group, NASA, the Office of the Comptroller of the Currency, and the United States Navy.

New directions and trends in coaching best practices were striking in these exemplary recent presentations:

- Intel—presented a study citing an ROI of its coaching program of more than 600 percent;
- Goldman Sachs—links coaching to specific business goals;
- Weyerhaeuser—the key role played by coaching in a rapid transformation and new identity for the sales organization;
- Wachovia—expects tight partnerships of internal HR and external coaching providers;
- GE and American Family Insurance—developed an internal coaching cadre of HR and OD professionals;
- MTV—increasingly recognizes the significance of adult learning and development theory in informing their coaching program;
- Avon—as part of global talent management, it prefers only coaches whose work is results-guaranteed for high potentials;
- Hasbro—links coaching to off-site executive development and strategy seminars held at Dartmouth;
- Deloitte—now requires training in coaching skills for all of its partners;
- ABN/AMRO—trains line managers from their business units in coaching skills.

Going forward, seminars and forums will continue to keep pace with trends in the field of coaching. Themes frequently mentioned on evaluations include:

- What are the best coaching models? What are the implications of adult learning theory? Is there a physiological basis for good coaching methodologies? What is the connection between coaching and psychology?

- How do you effectively introduce a coaching program within a corporation, ensure consistency in global coaching programs, and create a coaching culture?
- The critical link of coaching to leadership development, talent management, organization design, and business strategy.
- Coaching credentials.
- When should internal coaches be used? In what situations are external coaches more effective?
- How do you match coach to coachee? How do you measure results, including ROI? What about the issue of confidentiality?
- Do women leaders require different approaches to coaching? Are there diversity and generational implications in coaching?

Based on our research, we know that executive coaching is not just a fad, but a permanent mainstay in the development marketplace. Sixty-three percent of organizations in this study expected to increase their use of coaching over the next five years. Nearly all the remaining companies plan to continue with their current spending, and only 2 percent plan to decrease their coaching budget.

The most encouraging statistic came from the *customers* of the process—the leaders themselves. Ninety-two percent of leaders who have been coached indicate they would hire one again when the time is right.

About the Book

This book will serve as the definitive guide and should be required reading for anyone responsible for designing and/or managing a corporate coaching program. It is written for leadership development practitioners, strategic HR, the talent management group, internal and executive coaches, as well as for executives and leaders seeking to make the most of their coaching experiences.

The vast majority of learnings and examples could be applied to any industry, company, or organization. Likewise, the examples and experiences could occur in large, mid-size, or small organizations; private or publicly held firms; government entities; or start-up or established companies.

This book offers a robust 3-D view of the industry, depicting the similar and contradictory perspectives of organizations, coaches, and leaders. No other publication on the market today can make this claim. This information is invaluable in its contribution to a holistic approach to coaching and the evolution of the industry. Although the book approaches the coaching field from the viewpoint and experience of the three authors, it is influenced by the research study and participation of organizations that have contributed feedback, callouts, and insight into their company's practices.

We invite you as the reader to join the author, coaches, and practitioners from leading Fortune 1000 and Global 500 organizations in a journey to understand the state of the art in executive coaching and extend its impact in the business world.

Yes, coaching has clearly come of age.

1 • Understanding the Coaching Field

The word *coach* derives from 15th-century Hungary,[1] referring to the village of Kocs, where fine transportation coaches were first constructed. The purpose of a coach was to transport people from where they were to where they wanted to go.

Similarly, executive coaches facilitate the transportation of leaders to new levels of development and effectiveness. The optimal conditions for the journey include an integrated organizational system and human resources (HR) or leadership development (LD) practitioners to facilitate the journey, a coach trained and appropriate for the job, and a leader eager (or at least willing) to be transported somewhere.

A good place to start is to set the executive coaching foundation and build from there. What is coaching? Why do coaching? Who receives coaching? We'll take a further look into these basics in this chapter.

What Is Coaching?

Scroll through the academic, consulting, and other literature and you will find about as many definitions of executive coaching as there are coaches in the marketplace. Here are a few examples:

> *The essence of executive coaching is helping leaders get unstuck from their dilemmas and assisting them to transfer their learning into results for the organization.*[2]—Mary Beth O'Neil

> *Action coaching is a process that fosters self-awareness and that results in the motivation to change, as well as the guidance needed if change is to take place in ways that meet organizational needs.*[3]
> —Dotlich and Cairo

> *A helping relationship formed between a client who has managerial authority and responsibility in an organization and a consultant who uses a wide variety of behavioral techniques and methods to help the client achieve a mutually identified set of goals to improve his or her professional performance and personal satisfaction and, consequently to improve the effectiveness of the client's organization within a formally defined coaching agreement.*[4]—Kilberg

> *Executive Coaching is a one-on-one training and collaborative relationship between a certified or self-proclaimed coach and an executive interested in improving him- or herself primarily in career or business related skills.*[5]
> —Wikipedia, today's leading "Web 2.0" resource for user-generated content

We see executive coaching much more simply and offer this definition:

> Executive coaching is the one-to-one development of an organizational leader.

Executive coaching is *one leader, one coach.* The purpose is the development of the leader's skills, and executive coaching is intended for organizational leaders (whether or not they are in actual leadership positions). It doesn't matter if the company is large or small; for profit or nonprofit; private, governmental, or publicly held—the purpose remains the same.

Most emerging disciplines face a great variation in definitions. But there is no doubt that the practice of executive coaching is here permanently, regardless of how it is defined.

The Purpose of Coaching—Why?

Many leaders believe that they need to *get a coach,* without fully understanding *why* they need one. Plenty of organizations are guilty of this, too.

What is the point of coaching? Why do companies hire coaches?

At conference presentations, we often meet corporate practitioners asking about the different types of coaching. The confusion is understandable—there are lots of reasons to hire a coach. One executive development manager put it this way: "Executive coaching could be anything from building and sustaining leadership capacity, which is very difficult in these challenging times—to an executive with a leadership issue that needs remediation—to a leader in transition who is moving into a new role."

The top reason companies hire coaches is to develop the leadership capabilities of their executives. In our research, organizations, leaders, and coaches unanimously agreed that this is the primary purpose of coaching.

On a much smaller scale, coaching is also used to enhance career development, fix performance problems, retain high-potential employees, and manage leadership transitions.

A company's human resources or leadership development group can be of tremendous help in identifying how coaching will be used and linking it to the company's business strategies.

Let's review the leading answers from the research regarding the purpose of coaching (Fig. 3).

Leadership Development

Our study findings confirmed *leadership development* to be the clear purpose of most coaching engagements. The good news is that organizations and coaches were in nearly exact agreement regarding this point. They ranked leadership development the clear winner and agreed on the relative importance of the remaining options.

Leader Transition

Leader transitions, such as promotions, lateral moves, or international assignments, are all coaching opportunities. The scarcity of leadership talent combined with the rapid international expansion of many organizations requires leaders to make successful transitions quickly.

Playing off the success of *The First 90 Days*[6] and other books, more organizations are using coaches to facilitate leader transitions. One organization explained that they are now "doing some coaching around transitions and promotions or movements in the organization when we send somebody off on an expatriate assignment."

Other firms automatically assign a coach when a major transition occurs. One company says, "We use coaching as a development strategy, oftentimes aligned with new leader transitions—those who are stepping up into a new

Figure 3.   Purpose of coaching—organization, leader, and coach perspectives.

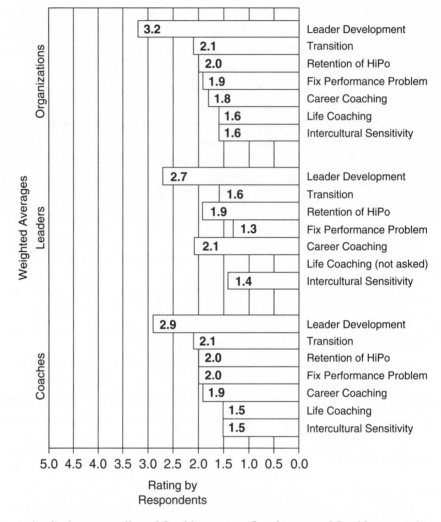

(scale: 1 = not at all used for this purpose; 5 = always used for this purpose)

role—to make sure that they are set up for success in that important first year."

We expect that more companies will begin to use coaching to help leaders transition between positions, with new promotions, or to help them during orientation (*on-boarding*) to a new environment. For example, Thrivent Financial for Lutherans has made good use of coaches during on-boarding transitions.

Using Coaches for Transitions

Kristin Olsen
*Thrivent Financial
for Lutherans*

At Thrivent Financial for Lutherans we use executive coaches as part of our *Start Right* program—our roadmap for on-boarding new senior sales leaders. *Start Right* has two key components that make up what we refer to as the 100-day plan—the development and initial implementation of a business plan for their region, and the identification and launching of their new team. An executive coach is provided to help support the execution of the plan and to create and begin the implementation of an individual development plan. The coach is in place for the first six months post-transition.

Transitions often involve a geographic move. We provide a coach in the area where they now live; an added benefit providing an opportunity to learn more about and build relationships in their new city.

Initially, we took the approach that individuals could choose whether they would have an executive coach. But over time we have learned it is such an important element of their future success that we now require it. We typically provide information to new leaders about the transition coaching process and their coach within a few weeks of being named to their new role. We choose a coach for them, with the option of switching if the relationship isn't working. This simplifies the process and gets the coach in place more quickly.

A fundamental step in the formation of the relationships is conversation between executive coaches and the sponsors/managers of individuals. The purpose of these calls is to provide the coaches with background about the nature of transition and key information that can contribute to the effectiveness of coaching. Because the leaders are in new positions and often *don't know what they don't know*, these conversations save time and contribute to the coaches' understanding of their work and our organization.

The executive coach provides reinforcement at a time when derailing is a real possibility by ensuring that these two areas remain a top priority. The coach is essentially our secondary support system and safety net to ensure that the individual stays on track during this crucial time in his or her career.

High-Potential Retention

Many companies have realized the value of coaching for leadership development as a means of retaining executives. Offering coaching is viewed as demonstrating the company's commitment to developing key leaders and internal talent. Leaders recognize the company's investment in their success and appreciate receiving this individual attention.

It's a win-win situation for both the leader and the company. The leader wins by receiving individual attention and increased developmental opportunity. The company wins with a faster-developing leader who is stronger, contributing to both current and future business. Several leaders we've met over the years credit coaching specifically as the reason they've stayed at their firms.

Performance Issues

In the early years, coaching was more often to correct an employee's performance who had gotten off track (*derailing*). In some organizations, it is still used in this way. But the trend, and most certainly the desire of practitioners, is to use coaching as infrequently as possible for performance issues.

Many companies have decided that other performance management practices are more appropriate for correcting poor performance, and they now reserve coaching—and its investment costs—for stronger performers. One organization says that, "One of the biggest changes that we have been able to institute over the last five years is moving executive coaching from a remedial to a development tool."

Companies that still use coaching to address performance problems may find a lack of interest in coaching from their star performers. Our recommendation is to discontinue the practice of performance problem coaching and reserve executive coaching only for those with bright futures at the company.

Career Coaching

Career coaching is primarily about assisting an individual with an assessment of where their career is now and where it may go next. This coaching is paid for by either individuals themselves or a company. Some well-known career management consultancies are now offering individualized coaching to support their efforts.

Leaders ranked *career coaching* as most frequently used after leadership development. Whereas companies want to use coaching for developing leaders, leaders also view coaching as a tool to personally enhance their individual careers. Interviewed leaders offered many comments about how the coaching experience played such a major role in their career development.

Many coaching programs exercise tight control regarding the purpose of coaching and the number of hours allocated to achieve that purpose. Coaching programs may enhance leader support by allowing a place and funds for such conversations during the engagement. One leader told us, "I think what a coach provides to me is a mirror—and facilitates me solving my own problems. I feel like I will always want a coach to work on my own development."

Life Coaching

Life coaching focuses on assisting clients to set and achieve goals in other aspects of their life rather than focusing exclusively on business objectives. In these cases, people choose areas of their life to improve, such as obtaining a personal goal (i.e., overcoming a financial or physical challenge), successfully making changes or transitions (i.e., career planning or relationship changes), or helping them manage a part of their life better (i.e., stress or time management).

Life coaching is not therapy, and these coaches are not therapists—although therapists may also be life coaches. Life coaching is almost always funded by the individual.

We believe that the coaching industry is currently at a crossroads; life coaching and executive coaching will likely diverge into separate industries. Each would offer distinct practices, certification requirements, and unique value propositions to their respective customers.

Content-Specific Coaching

At times, coaching is used to enhance traditional training programs. We've seen examples such as time management coaching, public speaking, financial literacy, communication skills, etc. Corporations use coaching in this way to continue the learning after the classroom training by adding follow-on coaching sessions.

General Mills offers coaching through a variety of different programs. They have found great success in their personal productivity coaching, as Kevin Wilde explains in the following excerpt.

Getting Things Done: Personal Productivity Coaching

Kevin Wilde
General Mills

General Mills provides coaching through three avenues: strategic leadership development coaching (associated with a program for the CEO and senior team), a coaching *clearinghouse* for individual assignments, and Getting Things Done (personal productivity coaching). It is the latter that has garnered particular attention for its innovative and successful approach to coaching.

Specific coaching in personal productivity is known as Getting Things Done. The program was designed by David Allen, author of the book by the same name. The focus is on helping executives be more productive in the workplace.

Coaching is built around a two-day office experience. An external coach and the leader review the basic concepts of the productivity methodology. The remainder of the time is spent applying practices with the most impact for the executive. The work often includes going through the entire office, collecting e-mails, paper, voice mails, and organizing everything into a workable system. The administrative assistant is often in attendance to support the leader.

As part of the follow-up process, coaching touchpoints are then built in for up to two years. A number of internal support processes have evolved that help executives continue their application. For example, 12 trained internal coaches often provide touch-up sessions to reinforce and extend the productivity practice for executives.

The program is incredibly popular as a career competitive edge or for those trying to achieve a better work–life balance. Coaches are assigned to leaders, as opposed to letting a leader choose, because the work is more about content than about chemistry. A small and nimble number of David Allen coaches handle the various leadership layers well.

Approximately 200 to 225 executives receive some form of training or coaching in a typical year. Of those, roughly 25 are engaged in Getting Things Done coaching yearly. The program has continued its increase in popularity. An internal staff of specialists will continue its support of the program, reinforcing the concepts among the recipients.

What Does Coaching Replace?

Coaching plays a growing role in the total arsenal of development options. In the Web research, 86 percent of the responding organizations indicated that coaching represents up to nearly a third of their total development offering. Leaders rated coaching even higher, with 91 percent also attributing nearly a third of their development to coaching.

What are generally considered the alternatives to executive coaching? Figure 4 shows the available options named by organizations and leaders. The three most popular answers from organizations were traditional internal training, mentoring, and developmental job assignments.

Leaders prioritized these alternatives differently. Although they agreed on internal training and external training, leaders placed a much lower priority on developmental job assignments (25% difference) and mentoring (37% difference) than organizations did.

With the growth of coaching, we believe that executive coaching will more regularly substitute for some of the more traditional methods over time. This would mean a shift from more general education to personal, one-on-one development.

Who Gets Coaching?

Many organizations are trying to determine which leaders should receive coaching. Should coaching be available only to vice presidents and above? To all executives? To high-potentials supporting the talent pool? Who would benefit the most?

A better question to ask is: What would have the greatest impact on the company—today and into the future? In our experience, this is best answered by considering three factors: the position level of the leader (today and in the future),

Figure 4.   Alternatives to executive coaching—organization and leader perspectives (select all that apply).

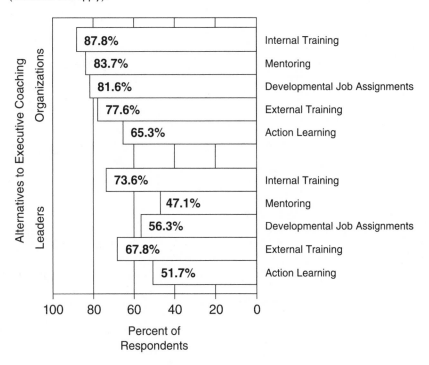

leader's performance and potential, and/or which leaders are most motivated to make the best use of coaching.

If coaching is new to your organization, use extreme care in determining which leaders would benefit first. These early adopters should be viewed as high-performing, highly influential leaders who will publicly endorse the value of their coaching experience. Building a coaching program from initial *performance problem* assignments sets a negative tone within the organization. It can be confusing to have a coaching program used for both poor performers and high achievers.

We looked at the level of leaders receiving coaching (Fig. 5). Vice-presidents are the most frequent customer group, then senior vice-presidents, followed by directors. This shows that coaching is still primarily reserved for executives in a company.

Surprisingly, high potentials were chosen in only about two-thirds (67%) of the companies. This suggests one great opportunity is to expand coaching programs to include high-potentials. As the future executives of tomorrow, companies would gain a great deal by dedicating resources to this group, thereby improving both retention and succession planning.

Figure 5.   What levels receive coaching?—organization perspective (select all that apply).

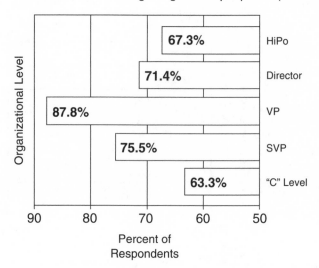

Also interesting was the number of organizational interviewees who did not know their company's general statistics. In many companies coaching is a decentralized activity. As a result, interviewees indicated they did not know these figures, or that they could comment only from the perspective of their own division, group, geography, etc.

As said at the outset, coaches facilitate the transportation of leaders from where they are to where they want to go. This process begins with being clear about the definition of coaching, its purpose, and who should get it.

Coaching Highlights

There are many definitions for coaching. Simply put, *Executive coaching is the one-to-one development of an organizational leader.* Ideally, coaching includes an integrated system with human resources or leadership development practitioners to facilitate the journey, a coach trained and appropriate for the job, and a leader eager to be transported.

- **Define coaching's purpose**. Be clear about the definition of coaching, its purpose, and who should receive it. The top reason companies hire coaches is to develop the leadership capabilities of their executives. On a much smaller scale, coaching is also used to enhance career development, fix performance problems, retain high-potential employees, and manage leadership transitions.
- **Decide where coaching will have the greatest impact**. Consider three factors: the level of the leader (today and in the future), leadership performance and potential, and/or which leaders are the most motivated.

- **Avoid using coaching for performance issues**. Building a coaching program from initial *performance problem* assignments sets a negative tone within the organization. It can be confusing to have a coaching program used for both poor performers and high achievers.
- **Leverage the company's human resources and/or leadership development group.** These professionals can be of tremendous help in identifying how coaching will be used and linking it to the company's business strategies.

2 • The Importance of Culture and Leadership Support

The success of coaching is strongly influenced by culture and leadership.

That isn't a surprise—but culture and leadership are sorely underestimated far too often. Coaching efforts can be greatly undermined by these two factors, no matter the size of the organization.

In some organizations, coaching is perceived very positively, with leaders asking for coaches and actively engaging in the process. There are often more leaders asking for coaching than the organization is able, or willing, to provide. Leaders are proud to have been chosen to receive executive coaching and they see it as a sign of the company's commitment to their career and future.

At the other end of the spectrum, coaching is either secretive or nonexistent. Coaching requests are few—and usually intended only for those in danger of transitioning out of the organization. Coaches are asked not to visit on site and meetings are conducted in secret. Leaders do not discuss their learnings, let alone their improvement areas, and may even downplay the coaching completely.

In screening new coaching requests, we often ask, "What is the history of coaching at your company? How do people feel about being asked to participate in a coaching program?" This gives us a preliminary read into the company's culture and leadership's acceptance of coaching.

This chapter looks at the impact of culture and leadership support on coaching initiatives and suggests how to respond when these factors are less than supportive.

Culture Counts

The most pervasive, yet perhaps the least appreciated dynamic in organizations is corporate culture. An organization's culture significantly guides the way decisions are made on a daily basis. We think of culture as the personality of the company, and as such, it influences how people behave.

Our research discovered how significant organizational culture is in supporting coaching. Those organizations with well-developed coaching approaches often cited their culture's natural support of people development and, in turn, coaching. In these companies, development is a natural part of work life. Leaders also view coaching as a positive benefit and not something to be done secretly.

Representative examples come from three key companies. One tells us, "In terms of the linkage to leadership development, coaching kind of fits the culture here. We have a culture that is relatively individualistic, and most executive learning really happens one-on-one." Another concurs: "Our culture is one that is very much supportive of coaching. Our CEO has someone who coaches him regularly." A third agrees, saying "We've gotten coaching ingrained as part of the culture in our organization because it has been a process that has been in place over time. We're now in our eighth year of doing this, so people understand it and buy into it."

In contrast, we've received calls over the years from leadership development professionals looking to bring coaching into their organizations—but with little cultural support. These practitioners know and understand the power of coaching, but they find themselves in organizations where coaching—and people development—is not easily accepted by the culture. These practitioners will often ask how to create a coaching culture.

In one case, a new company president sought coaching, but he agonized over how to describe the situation to his peers. He spent more than 30 minutes with us on the phone perfecting his spin on coaching. He wanted his peers to know that *he*—not his organization—had asked for coaching, to show he wasn't in trouble.

Organizations of all sizes are advised to conduct an honest analysis of their cultural attitude toward development and then determine how to build the coaching approach. Often this information is already available through historical investment in development, culture surveys, or exit interview data.

If coaching is not a natural fit, we recommend several options for these challenging cultures.

- Find the path of least resistance. Start by coaching a specific leader or department who seems to understand the value of it.
- Locate a high-profile executive sponsor to underwrite the effort.
- Introduce coaching as an add-on to other development training programs.

- Offer coaching to a new leader entering the organization who may be less reticent.

One insurance company we have worked with introduced coaching at the bottom of the organization, hoping that success at that level would make coaching more interesting to senior leadership.

Companies have to start somewhere. After coaching begins, it often becomes accepted and then ingrained in the organization over time.

Further advice on corporate culture is offered by seasoned practitioner Sam Humphrey of Unilever. She advises analyzing culture on three levels: individual, team, and organizational.

Culture Counts— How We Do Things 'Round Here

Sam Humphrey
Unilever

When implementing coaching in an organization, one should consider the organization's culture through three lenses: the individual lens, the team lens, and the organizational lens. Each lens may have a different perspective on a number of the key success components, and if each lens views each of these components differently, then the coaching intervention is unlikely to work.

For example, let's assume that the key success component is identifying the purpose of the coaching. The individual lens sees coaching as a developmental intervention, whereas the team views coaching as remedial. The organization may see coaching for improved performance. This scenario is unlikely to yield great results. The expectations of each group will dictate their thoughts and actions from this point on, emphasizing the importance of alignment.

When introducing coaching to an organization, one should consider coaching within the context of the current culture.

At the individual level, one might look for:

- How much freedom to be themselves do individuals believe they have?
- What's in it for an individual to be coached?
- How well have previous team/personal development interventions worked for individuals?
- How coachable are individuals?

At the team level, one might look for:

- What type of support have teams here given to individuals going through a change or development?
- What's in it for the team to have a member coached?

At the organizational level, one might look for:

- How will coaching be measured?
- How is individual or team change rewarded and recognized?
- How will matching be handled (by choice, or by assigned coaches)?
- Who is the client—the individual being coached, or the organization?

At the heart of this issue is alignment. If there is cultural alignment between each of these three perspectives regarding why coaching is being introduced, what purpose it will serve, and how it will be measured, then coaching stands a much higher chance of success.

Teaching leaders to coach can be a key aspect of fostering a coaching culture. Harris Ginsberg shares his experiences in this effort.

Coaching as a Corporate Learning Intervention

Harris Ginsberg
Chemtura Corporation

What happens when coaching becomes a cornerstone of a leadership development strategy? One large technology company invested in leadership coaching for its 300 senior leaders. Over a five-year period, leaders improved their understanding and skill in coaching their direct reports. Coaching—as a process and a mindset—became woven into succession planning, high-potential talent development, and leadership development programs.

Sound far-fetched? Perhaps, but many companies have taken similar paths in their application of coaching as one among many learning strategies. The technology giant selected internal and external coaches who learned a common *leadership framework* that integrated behavior and values, business strategy, and organization development. These leadership consultants applied that framework in coaching the senior executives on personal leadership, advising them on organizational issues, and working *in the trenches* with leaders on the practice of leadership. In most cases, 360° feedback on a set of leadership competencies and dimensions of organizational climate formed the basis for the intervention.

In addition, high-potential participants in executive development programs received coaching as part of their action learning. Executive coaching underscored the commitment to high-potential leadership candidates rather than to remediation for mediocre or average performers.

Finally, the company examined the qualities of coaches to identify a standard of best practices. The best coaches demonstrated the following categories of behaviors:

- Engaging in a coaching conversation
- Developing the relationship

- Communicating effectively
- Facilitating learning and results

In addition, they identified additional capabilities of external and internal coaches that would enhance their impact on leaders:

- Business savvy and industry knowledge
- Organizational change
- Ethics (as defined by APA, SIOP)
- Knowledge of leadership and executive leadership development

Coaching became an expectation of managers and a differentiator in performance management. Ultimately, managers were held accountable for performance coaching of their direct reports. Creating a culture that embraces coaching requires perseverance and clear accountability for professional coaches, human resources and learning professionals, and managers. Coaching can effectively impact performance and culture when applied as an integrated component of a learning strategy.

More organizations are looking to do what Harris is suggesting—training leaders to be better coaches in the context of their jobs. This will have a positive impact on the organizational culture.

Get Leadership Support

Highly successful coaching initiatives will nearly always include the support of senior management. Just as with any corporate effort—strategic, operational, or developmental—senior leadership support is critically important. Although it is possible to have a successful coaching program without strong support, it is a lot easier with it.

Most successful corporate practitioners cite CEOs or senior leaders as recipients of coaching. Of course, these executives will also be primary influencers of the company culture's support of coaching.

Many well-respected CEOs are coachees. They speak publicly about the value of working with a coach to further their development. Coaching initiatives at these firms are significantly easier to roll out among leaders. As one organization told us, "The primary reason coaching is well accepted is because our CEO has had this guy he has been using for a time, and others have jumped on the band wagon to say 'Well, if he uses one, it's okay for me to use one.'"

Negative Stigma Still?

Organizations indicated that about 43 percent of CEOs have received coaching. In additon, 71 percent of the organizations indicated that at least one member of their executive team had received coaching. These numbers are encouraging testimony for coaching.

However, these statistics were challenged when we asked whether these same individuals *publicly endorsed* coaching. Six percent fewer CEOs and 22 percent fewer executive team members were willing to do so (Fig. 6). Interestingly, whereas fewer CEOs retain a coach than senior executives (43% vs. 71%), CEOs are proportionally more willing to endorse coaching than are members of their executive team!

Figure 6.   Senior leaders who receive and endorse coaching—organization perspective.

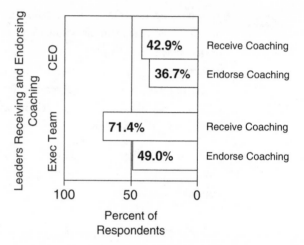

Some negative perception still exists, evidently. Senior executives worry that having a coach means they are showing weakness, their job performance is in trouble, or they are on their way out. In our many years of screening coaching requests, we've met leaders like these. They ask for shorter coaching assignments, avoid meeting their coach in public, or call it consulting. As one such company told us, "Our CEO endorses coaching—but not publicly."

We routinely ask organizations, "Whose idea was it to hire a coach?" In this way, we can get an idea of the coachee's attitude or interest toward coaching. In some cases, the executives do not yet know that coaching is being recommended to them. This gives coaches a warning of potential lack of interest in the assignment.

A creative strategy to raise desirability of coaching is to foster a perception of exclusivity by informing potential leaders that they have been *specially selected* to receive coaching. Leader interest and commitment can be bolstered by this clever strategy.

At Sony, leadership support has become embedded in a culture through Leadership Forum sessions held throughout the year. The Forums focus solely on high-potential leaders.

Leadership Forum

Deborah Swanson

Sony Corporation

One successful initiative at Sony has been a Leadership Forum with seven sessions and follow-up conducted over several months. It is a four-day leadership development workshop for managers, directors, and vice-presidents who have been identified as high-potential leaders. Each session averages 20 participants; a total of 128 participated in 2005. High-potential talent pool members are identified across all businesses and invited to attend the Forum by the President.

Each Forum includes senior business head participation in both the design of our custom business simulations and the delivery of important business updates. In addition to the work done at the Forum, teams continue to work together over a ten-week execution phase by applying what they learned to real job and business initiatives.

Executive coaches embedded during the Leadership Forum assist in offering guidance and structured group peer coaching. Their role is to observe and then provide feedback to both individuals and teams. In addition, the coaches provide a summary to both the Forum participants and the senior leadership team in attendance.

This four-day program is an intense effort designed to help leaders understand the impact of their leadership behavior on the company's bottom line. Each team reports out what they have learned during the Forum and offers suggestions to the senior leaders on the last day. At the close of every program, each leader identifies two personal learning goals to ensure that his or her learning continues over the ten-week execution phase.

Although the primary focus of the Forums is on the development of high-potential leaders, the interaction among participants has also produced many ideas and led to the implementation of these new improvements. A virtual wrap-up session at the end of ten weeks allows leaders to report back to executives on the progress they've made, creates accountability on the part of the leader, and allows executives to hear first-hand about the value of learning and its real bottom-line impact.

A successful program such as Sony's, which includes highly regarded leaders throughout the company, will win supporters for leadership development and coaching.

Why Is Coaching Different?

Coaching offers a rare opportunity for a leader to receive one-on-one attention. It is a way for the company to make a personal commitment to the individual's development.

Accordingly, the coachee may at first feel uneasy or uncertain about it. If your coaching program is new or not well-known, someone needs to make sure that the leader understands the purpose of the work and what to expect. Helping the leader understand what will happen is important to ensure a positive experience.

In the following section, Zeynep Tozum challenges us to think about what is possible with leadership development and coaching.

What's Growing Ourselves Through Coaching Got to Do with Growing Our Business?

Zeynep Tozum
FARBEYOND Consulting

Breaking through limitations and sustaining new territory is exactly what leads to new business creation and growth. How amazingly similar to what an individual experiences on his or her path to growth!

Beyond the obvious structural changes, growth of a business actually requires an attitude adjustment. Consequently, leaders need to reinvent *themselves* while rethinking the business. Getting there is not magic, but the result of work that leads to alignment, purposeful action, and creativity.

Coaching can truly be a practical tool to help grow the business, significantly accelerating the process for individuals and teams to see new possibilities and deliver with greater speed. The coach can be instrumental in helping leaders help themselves to grow in a variety of ways:

Choosing and committing to a purpose. As leaders, stretching ourselves with new ways of responding and behaving can generate creative tension and some discomfort. What will ease this discomfort is the notion of *purpose*. The coach helps the leader articulate an exciting purpose that has the potential to make a difference in business results and build awareness and commitment around the challenges it involves. The coach will look for that commitment to anchor the leader's work.

Building clarity of what is so. We are blind to many of our qualities, as well as to our dysfunctional behaviors and limiting beliefs. Gathering and assimilating feedback about ourselves and the systems we live in is key to personal development. Coaching can effectively support and enhance this process of heightening awareness.

Learning through practice. Rather than offering solutions, the coach helps the leader dare to look at inner resistance, to understand consequences, to find new strategies, and to practice—thus stretching beyond current limitations for new behaviors.

In summary, considering yourself to be a project in service of the growth you want to create in your business makes you feel awake, full of choices, and powerful. This work, especially when supported by coaching, can alter the *substance* of how you lead, beyond a mere change in form. This is how a soft concept such as personal growth can stand right at the hard end of performance.

Reminding our leaders that their development does carry a link to the development of the business is a regular responsibility of strategic human resources and leadership development practitioners.

Marketing Matters

The marketing of coaching programs requires proper consideration. A coaching effort needs to reach the radar screen of prospective customers: potential coachees, their managers, local HR support staff, and regional LD people.

At one client corporation, an HR generalist called us seeking a coach for an executive. She said, "It took me forever to find information on my company's coaching program. It was really more by luck that I figured out where to call to get connected to coaches."

We weren't surprised. This company had been facing financial and structural challenges and had greatly reduced its attention to coaching over the past few years. Marketing of coaching was no longer a priority.

Marketing efforts we've seen involve some of the following:

- Launch a kickoff forum to introduce the coaching program to various customer segments.
- Create an intranet site with program details; include links to this site from other key spots on the intranet (e.g., one's online career profile).
- Review coaching program updates during regular human resources and/or leadership development update calls.
- Select supportive and influential leaders to pilot the program. Ensure that they publicly discuss their development and coaching goals.
- Collect endorsement statements from coached leaders. Post these, with their pictures, on the intranet and through marketing avenues.
- Aggregate coach satisfaction data (*see* Chapter 8) that can be included in marketing materials.
- Summarize and publicize leadership improvement feedback, such as a mini-survey (*see* Chapter 8).
- Secure positive publicity with success stories featured in corporate publications, both internal and external.
- Write articles and present your corporate case study in industry venues. Use reprints of these efforts in marketing materials.

• Invite human resources and leadership development staff to coach gatherings, such as conference calls or all-coach meetings. After meeting coaches face-to-face, we've found a noticeable increase in the utilization of those coaches by LD and HR representatives.

Also, consider how other development efforts are marketed in your organization. What works and what does not? Apply those learnings to this campaign.

In some organizations, marketing may be counterproductive as the result of a tightly controlled selection process. Coaching is reserved for a limited number of leaders. Beware that alerting everyone to a coaching effort will draw leaders who may not qualify because of their organizational level or their ranking in the talent management system. The organization is then in the uncomfortable position of explaining why coaching is being denied.

Coaching Highlights

The purpose of this chapter has been to reinforce the importance of culture and leadership support. In our experience, the most successful practitioners recognize and account for these factors. It is not impossible to navigate coaching-unfriendly cultures, but it is much easier when the potential pitfalls are identified. Every coaching program needs internal marketing as well, so don't overlook that effort.

• **Culture counts.** Learn about the company's cultural view. Ask key questions, such as "What is the history of coaching at our company? How do people feel about being asked to participate in a coaching program?"

• **Be clear about the purpose.** Coaching offers a rare opportunity for a leader to receive one-on-one attention and to make a personal commitment to an individual's development. If your coaching program is new or not well-known, be sure that the leader understands the purpose of the work and what to expect to ensure a positive experience.

• **Be stealth-like, if needed.** In non-supportive cultures, offer coaching first for the most interested leaders, find an executive sponsor, add coaching to other training programs, or offer coaching to newly transitioning leaders.

• **Boost the image.** Don't allow coaching to be used for performance problems; this will degrade the view of coaching for more promising leaders. Instead, position coaching as an exclusive benefit only for specially selected leaders. Even offer coaching "by invitation only."

• **Marketing matters.** A robust coaching marketing plan is helpful: How have other efforts been successfully marketed internally? Find the right leaders to go first, publicize positive testimonials and impact data, and promote the program to internal HR and LD.

3 • Linking Coaching to Leadership Development, Talent Management, and Human Resource Practices

The evolution of coaching requires organizations to link coaching to their leadership development and talent management goals.

Whereas the leadership development strategy identifies *how* to develop leaders, the talent management approach identifies *who* should be developed, and *when*. Coaching can be a strong supporter of both the *who* and the *how* of connecting leader development to an organization's strategies and goals. However, without the link coaching may become a haphazard, hit-or-miss intervention, with a lower probability of successfully maximizing its benefits.

It is important for any organization to discuss the role of coaching in supporting leadership development and talent management. This ties the purpose and results of the coaching to the strategy and positions the company for the future. In one good example, an organization told us that "Executive coaching provides tailored development for selected executives to help address important issues—succession to the next level, key transitions, ongoing development—and addresses a potential derailer. It accelerates development of current leaders [to] ensure that we have the talent in place to achieve business objectives."

In general, organizations have done a better job of linking coaching to leadership development than to talent management. The next needed step is a clear connection between the talent pool and succession planning. Only the most sophisticated coaching programs maintain some type of system via software or a human resource information system (HRIS) that includes succession planning profiles of leaders.

This chapter takes a look at some of the key linkages between coaching and leadership development strategies or talent management systems. Additionally, we will clarify the supporting roles for both leadership development and human resources staff.

Link to the Leadership Development Strategy

Organizations that create leadership development approaches linked to company strategies have answered key questions, such as: What is our business strategy? and, How do we develop leaders capable of executing our strategy?

Our research found that most organizations are interested in better integrating coaching with their leadership development strategies, rather than handling coaching requests in an ad hoc manner.

In one example, the senior VP for human resources at an energy company contacted us to find a coach for a top executive. However, this 20-year-old company had a limited history of leadership development and did not have a current plan for its use in the future. We encouraged the SVP to consider establishing a leadership development strategy prior to haphazardly throwing coaching at problems. Given the challenges in their industry—and the executives' lack of readiness for these challenges—coaching one executive would not be sufficient.

Sadly, this organization went into bankruptcy a year later. Although a missing leadership development strategy was not the culprit, it is possible that better-developed leaders might have helped the company survive.

A recognized standard in selecting leadership development approaches would be to follow the 70/20/10 guideline suggested by the Center for Creative Leadership (CCL).[1] This guideline states that 70 percent of a leader's learning derives from actual work experience; 20 percent is on-the-job learning; and 10 percent is from formal education and training.

Coaching and mentoring are included in the 20 percent that is on-the-job learning. Thus, organizations following this model will not rely solely on coaching—or any other intervention—for leader development. They will integrate different modes according to a model such as CCL's.

Many organizations believe that they have satisfactorily linked executive coaching activities to their leadership development strategies. In our research, 96 percent of the organizations feel that their coaching effort is *somewhat linked* or *highly linked* to their leadership development strategies. These organizations have crafted an overall strategy toward developing leaders and have determined how coaching fits within that strategy.

The majority of organizations have identified leadership competencies that are critical to their future. These competencies usually are accompanied by behavioral statements assessed with a 360-degree feedback tool. Coaches working in these companies are frequently asked to help leaders develop these key competencies.

Finally, some companies have developed resource guides in the form of either hard copy or online tools to provide leaders with guidance on how to improve in specific competencies. These guides offer specific key activities, recommended readings, trainings, and other resources. We recommend coaches have access to these guides and use them in assisting leaders in their specific areas for development.

Linking to the Talent Management Approach

One of the benefits to having an established coaching or leadership development program is the pipeline of well-prepared leaders. Organizations are generally much less prepared than they would prefer to be.

In contrast to the link to leadership development strategies, only 71 percent of organizations felt their coaching approach was *somewhat linked* or *highly linked* to their talent management strategy. One interviewee explained it well, saying, "Our talent management strategy is … being reinvigorated … coaching sort of fits and is not as robustly connected with other initiatives as it probably should be." Another indicated that the company's talent management strategy "is now in early stages, but coaching is an obvious tool we will use within."

Linking a coaching approach to a company's talent management strategy, therefore, presents an improvement opportunity for many organizations. As a whole, companies are not well prepared when it comes to thoughtful, robust talent management systems. A 2005 Executive Development Associates study[2] found that a vast majority of firms had not established talent management systems, even though they faced unprecedented talent shortages in the coming years.

Firms that have good talent management links are better able to determine which leaders should receive coaching, and when. They can more easily determine how much coaching different leaders should receive and which coaching topics would best benefit each leader. Some will advocate a tailored approach for each leader to apply towards coaching and other development budget activities.

Usually, these organizations will be using coaching solely for those high-potential or high-performing leaders, reserving other options for performance problems. As one organizational interviewee explained, "Coaching is integrated into the annual talent management process. All executive coaching is approved by the line manager and included in the individual's IDP (individual development plan)."

We found that coaches were surprisingly aware of the talent management approaches of their client companies. Coaches indicate a strong preference for a strategically linked coaching approach, rather than one-off, haphazard assignments. When coaches are aware of the company's approach and strategies, they are more likely to be successful.

"One of the prerequisites I place on my clients is that they have a strategic approach to coaching before they hire me," says one coach. "It is very important to me. In other instances, as I work with my clients, I help them transform their coaching programs into strategic initiatives."

Ensure that your leadership development strategy properly characterizes coaching as one of many development options, and that your talent management approach drives the process where these options—including coaching—are employed. Coaching development goals will be more effective when linked to the talent management system and tracked against progress.

In the following description, Sony shares how they use a Talent Management Council to determine which leaders should receive coaching.

Talent Management Council

Deborah Swanson
Sony Corporation

In 2003, a group of eight senior leaders representing our key businesses were brought together to form our Talent Management Council (TMC). Their initial role was to support the selection and development of our cross-functional high-potential leaders. They are responsible for the direction of our talent management and leadership development efforts, plus all major decisions related to talent initiatives. Council members review business unit nominations at the director level and above and make the final selection of our enterprise-wide talent pool. Another role is their involvement in teaching and providing business updates at our Leadership Forum, a weeklong workshop for talent pool members. After a ten-week application of learning goals on the job, TMC members also participate in a virtual wrap-up session to listen to actual results created.

In addition to participating in the selection process, the Talent Management Council meets quarterly to discuss issues, evolve the process, and provide governance over all leadership development programs centralized in one talent management budget. This provides common resources and developmental experiences to high potentials, including executive coaching, external programs for individual needs, and our internal leadership curriculum. An important recent initiative was to provide manager training on our Developing Sony Talent initiative to support the role of creating strong development plans and coaching.

One key to our success has been to position talent management and leadership development as a business process, not a human resources process. By involving business leaders across our siloed divisions, talent management occurs on a larger scale and ensures alignment with business strategies and goals.

The TMC meetings provide an opportunity to update business leaders on our talent pool status, align current leadership capabilities with business direction, review our efforts, and identify gaps in our leadership ranks. The Talent Management Council itself has also evolved. Initially a process to identify, develop, and get to know future leaders, it has evolved to focus now on cross-company and even global strategic moves to develop leaders and provide breadth of experience.

Linking to Leadership Development and Human Resources Personnel

Coaching has also impacted the roles of internal leadership development (LD) and human resources (HR) personnel. At times, it can be unclear as to what their role should be in regards to individual coaching assignments.

Usually the leadership development team does most of its work on the front end of a coaching engagement. They establish parameters for a coaching program and screen potential coaches and vendors. Leadership development staff may also prescreen potential assignments to ensure that coaching is the appropriate intervention. They may then recommend several coaches for an individual assignment.

Local, on-the-ground human resources personnel may also be involved with this same matching process, and they may provide feedback or insights to the coach as an assignment starts. The local HR person often becomes the primary client contact over the term of the assignment.

As Figure 7 illustrates, the role of leadership development and human resources is mostly evident on the front end—identifying coaching at the outset as the appropriate solution and assisting with the matching process. But we advise that HR and LD can play a strong role throughout the entire coaching process, not just in the beginning.

Figure 7.   Role of human resource and leadership development—organization, leader, and coach perspectives (select all that apply).

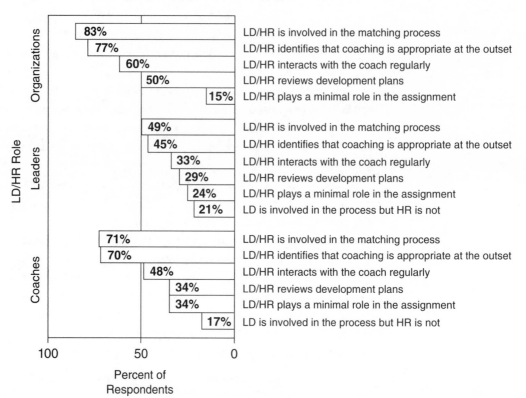

Notice that only 15 percent of organizations selected *LD/HR plays a minimal role in the assignment*, but 24 percent of leaders and 34 percent of coaches made the same selection. This indicates leaders and coaches do not necessarily perceive the full contribution of the LD/HR staff.

In large organizations, there could be inconsistencies within the company. As one coach observed, "In my experience, LD/HR does not act uniformly even in one organization. One division's LD/HR may be very involved and another may be less involved."

As a general rule, leaders and coaches appreciate the continued connection to assignments underway by LD/HR. From the leaders' perspective, organizations could do more to follow up after an assignment has begun. To improve coaching assignments, we recommend that LD and HR:

- Ensure a good match
- Verify leader satisfaction
- Ensure that the coach is properly oriented
- Measure impact
- Check in at the midpoint and the conclusion of assignments

Although these steps add to the overall workload, leaders and coaches appreciate them. The check-in can be automated by preprogramming touchpoint dates and prewritten check-in letters into a project management system.

As one leader who was satisfied with the support told us, "They have been really terrific—my training and development people—about checking in and asking about milestones during this process. So I give them very high marks for that."

LD or HR can also add great value by creating a *dossier* of materials for each new coaching assignment. It is helpful to provide the coach with previous 360 results, culture surveys, performance reviews, organizational charts, relevant executive bios, self-assessments, etc. This saves the coach and the leader from locating all of that information separately.

In the following example, Janet Matts illustrates one way an internal practitioner can get involved in coaching assignments. She describes what she calls her *white space* role at Johnson & Johnson. In that capacity, Janet plays a vital part in linking her company, leaders, and coaches together and supporting coaching assignments.

Working in the White Space

Janet Matts
Johnson & Johnson

With the responsibility for executive assessment and coaching for Johnson & Johnson, I serve as a liaison, advisor, and confidant to the leader being coached, to the leader's boss and HR support, and to the coach. It is very much a behind-the-scenes *connecting activity* that adds great value to the successful launch of an assignment, ensuring the sustainability of the work and increasingly creating a *coaching culture*.

The link can be directly with the leader requesting coaching, or in conversation with their HR connection. I can advise them or help their HR partner decide on whether coaching is right for them, how to make the most of coaching, and which coaches they should consider working with on assignment. I am connected with many of our coaches, and I can advise coaches on how to navigate successfully at J&J. As an executive coach myself in the Johnson & Johnson organization prior to taking on my current role, and as a 20-year J&J veteran, I am able to relate to what leaders do and what it takes to be part of such a complex environment.

I interface with HR in the organization where the leader is being coached, learning more about the bigger picture, connecting the coach with HR, and advising on the leader's progress. I use my experience, knowledge, and intuition to provide an HR VP or leadership director with the right coaches to be considered for their leader, and to help them build their own pool of coaches.

In order to be successful in such a role, one has to have great credibility and trust throughout the organization. One needs a deep understanding of the company's business and culture, credentials as a coach, and experience walking in the shoes of executive coaching. Establishing strict confidentiality parameters and boundaries with each constituency is required. One must be able to see the process through different lenses—as a leader, a coach, or an HR professional.

Triage coaching requests

Someone internally should play a *triage* role to screen coaching requests and ensure that coaching is the right intervention. The screener should have a set list of questions to ask—or the requestor can complete a form—to clarify the details surrounding the potential request. If coaching is not appropriate, the screener can then recommend alternative interventions for the request.

At Intel, screeners complete a form when someone requests a coach. An example of their form and types of questions to ask is shown in Figure 8.

Figure 8.   Intel coaching request screening sheet.[1]

Coaching Request Form

Name _____   Date _____

Current Position _____   Phone _____

Business Group _____   Manager _____

Location _____   Admin _____

- What are your expectations regarding the coaching interaction (i.e. what do you want to gain as a result of coaching):

- What business challenges are you currently facing today?

- What specific skills or competencies do you want to develop or improve further?

- Have you had previous coaching experience(s)? If so, please explain length of engagement, outcome or results.

- Have you taken a 360 feedback tool in the last 18 months?

- Do you have any specific coaching preferences? (i.e. specific background of coach, gender, geographic area, Intel experience)

- Any additional questions or concerns you would like answered?

The human resources or leadership development practitioner responsible for the coaching program is the ideal candidate to be the screener for coaching requests. One organizational practitioner who handles coaching requests explains that sometimes people "just ask for a list of coaches. I don't do that. There needs to be a conversation. Is coaching the right opportunity for them, and if not, where should I steer them?" She goes on to point out that people are usually very grateful for this extra level of screening, especially when coaching is not the right intervention.

Questions to consider in screening requests are shown in Table 2.

Table 2   Screening Triage Issues

QUESTION TO ASK	PURPOSE
What is the purpose for coaching?	To ensure the need matches your coaching program's capabilities
How is this leader viewed in the talent pool?	Clarifies if the leader is worth the investment
Whose idea was it to get a coach (the leader, their boss, HR)?	Gives insight into the leader's interest in coaching
Has this leader been told about coaching yet?	Clarifies leader interest; identifies "management by proxy" (see below)
What has the boss said to the leader about the coaching?	Ensures that leader and boss are aligned on the expectations and purpose of the coaching assignment
What else has been tried so far?	Provides information about previous efforts and outcomes
How long does this leader have to improve?	Unreasonably short time frame reveals performance management issue
What is the reputation or history of the boss when it comes to talent development?	Provides insight into likelihood of success and the role the boss will play
What support can the leader expect during coaching?	Sets the leader up for success and appropriate partnering for the coaching
What happens if this leader does not improve in the identified area?	If leader will be let go, a performance management issue is revealed

Discourage Management by Proxy

Management by proxy is when a boss wants someone else to deliver the message that a leader is not performing up to standard. We believe this is not a coach's role, and it should be avoided.

One general manager phoned us requesting 360-degree feedback for one of his direct reports. He was not interested in any coaching beyond a single feedback session. As we delved deeper into the boss's concerns, we had a suspicion that had to be tested.

"Have you discussed these concerns with your direct report?" we asked.

"Yes. Well, not in exactly the same way I just explained them to you," he answered. "Probably not quite as clearly. But I really need him to understand the impact his behavior has on everyone around him. The 360 should be able to send that message."

This leader was setting up a coach to deliver the feedback he was unable to do himself. Gathering this feedback in a 360-style assessment would bolster the message that *everyone thinks this way*. This is *management by proxy*—a tricky proposition for coaching.

Three indicators tip us off to management by proxy.

- First, watch for a boss interested in 360-degree feedback, but unwilling to invest in coaching beyond a single session. The hope is to get the message across without spending too much money.
- Second, if the boss is taking an abnormally active role in setting up coaching, such as personally calling coaching firms, screening coaches, or requiring excessive communication with the coach—be aware. The boss is likely under tightening pressure to finally deal with an incessant performance issue and feels the need to overly manage the entire process.
- Third—and usually only internal staff can do this—those familiar with the boss may already know his or her reputation in regard to handling performance problems. This can give internal staff a clue to the boss's history.

Coaching can still benefit the leader involved in this scenario. However, it is important that the boss properly manage performance issues prior to coaching. This is the boss's job as the manager, not the coach's.

In the above example, we asked the general manager to deliver the feedback before we would engage. We are thankful that we had a supportive leadership development partner strongly supporting our recommendation. We never heard back from the boss again.

Two ways to help manage coaching are with a series of checklists that enable consistency—especially in a large organization—and by actively managing the coaching relationship. In the following example, Kevin Wilde provides some practical advice for internal practitioners in charge of managing coaching.

Adding Value from the Inside: Actions to Support Coaching as an Internal Resource

Kevin Wilde
General Mills

As coaching grows, internal HR, OD, and leadership development professionals may be missing key actions that would enable them to make the most of their coaching investments.

One way for internal resources to become a stronger partner in the coaching process is to create a checklist of key milestones relevant to the company's coaching engagements. For example:

Checklist of expectation setting. Have I clarified expectations with the key stakeholders of this coaching engagement? Topics to include: What are we trying to improve? What is coaching supposed to deliver? Is coaching really the right solution?

Checklist of active management. Have I set a schedule of periodic check-ins with both the leader and the coach? Key questions to ask: How is coaching going? What outcomes have you achieved from coaching so far? How much follow-up with your manager and other stakeholders are you doing? What could be done to enhance the impact of your coaching investment?

Checklist of evaluating success. Have I managed the processes of closure and evaluating success? Topics to consider: What will be the standards to assess progress? What methods will we use? How will we bring closure to the project? What follow-up support and further check-ins might we consider?

The managing of key relationships is also critical to the success of the program. An internal resource is often in the best position to judge the various relationships in an ongoing coaching engagement. The internal resource should have developed relationships with each coach in the pool, preferably having met them in person at least once, with repeated ongoing interactions. It's also helpful to be familiar with each coach's background and style and to be capable of making educated coach recommendations that are appropriate to each new assignment.

As each assignment is underway, the internal resource should also build a strong relationship with the coachee. This is the opportunity to show active support for the process while being sensitive to the integrity of the contract.

The internal resource can add incredible value to the equation through these key actions, which will greatly enhance investment for a significant developmental opportunity.

This coaching process description from General Mills shows how internal practitioners can be strong partners, even when they are not the ones actually doing the coaching.

Connecting the dots begins with a clear vision of leadership development strategies, the talent management approach, and your company's human resource practices. A solid connection among them positions coaching for the best chance of success.

Coaching Highlights

The most successful coaching programs have a direct link to their leadership development and talent management goals. Examples of how to link coaching include Sony's Talent Management Council, the *white space* role described at Johnson & Johnson, and suggestions from General Mills on ways to link internal resources to coaching.

- **Identify the how, who, and when.** Whereas the leadership development strategy identifies *how* to develop leaders, the talent management approach identifies *who* should be developed, and *when*. Link coaching to both the *how* and the *who* to increase success and maximize its benefits.
- **Business strategy.** Address and answer key questions, such as, What is our business strategy? and, How do we develop leaders capable of executing our strategy?
- **Resource guides.** Develop resource guides that provide leaders guidance on how to improve in specific competencies; offer specific key activities; and suggest recommended readings, trainings, and other resources.
- **Human resources and leadership development roles.** HR and LD can play a strong role throughout the entire coaching process by:

  - Determining if coaching is the right intervention;
  - Screening coaching requests;
  - Ensuring a good match;
  - Verifying leader satisfaction;
  - Ensuring that the coach is properly oriented;
  - Measuring impact;
  - Checking in at the midpoint and the conclusion of assignments.

4 • Managing the Coaching Engagement

In the past several years, the coaching field has evolved enough that if someone says, "We would like a six-month coaching engagement," the meaning is increasingly understood. It isn't always a certainty though, so the utmost clarity of communication between organization, leader, and coach is still needed.

There are a lot of questions to answer about a coaching engagement. How many hours of coaching are needed, how often, and provided in what way? What instruments are included? What deliverables is the coach expected to produce? How are results measured? What does the coaching cost, and is it paid by the hour or by the project?

We predict that over the next few years the *standard coaching engagement* will move toward uniformity. As is typical in other maturing industries, buyers will know what an engagement entails and what the typical extras may be.

In an effort to advance coaching standards, we clarify many of these typical details, including leader and boss preparation, leader matching, assignment duration/mechanism/frequency, what happens during assignments, and cost.

Preparing the Executive for Coaching

One time we arrived at the first meeting with an executive who had already agreed to coaching. Everything was supposedly set up ahead of time by human resources. The contract was already signed. We shook hands and sat down.

"So you're a coach," the executive began. "What is a coach? Is it like a motivational speaker?" It was an uphill climb from that moment on.

Preparing executives for coaching is the responsibility of the corporate leadership development or human resources staff. The leader needs clear guidance on the purpose, activities, and outcomes of coaching. Leaders need to know what is expected of them, the time required, and who has access to what information. They should also know what executive coaching is *not* (i.e., a never-ending engagement, therapy, etc.)

We suggest that corporate staff should spend time with the leader to clarify coaching expectations. One idea is to create a coaching description document for executives that is posted on an internal Web site and shared at the time of initial inquiry. Articles describing the benefits of coaching can also be included in this package.

Through our research with coached leaders, coach and study researcher Sue Brown has gathered advice to help other leaders make the most of their coaching experience.

Leaders: Make the Most of Your Coaching

Sue Brown
*SJ Brown & Associates;
Study Researcher*

Executive leaders from Fortune 1000 and Global 500 companies were interviewed in our research. Their thoughts and comments on the coaching experience are summarized in the checklist below.

Coaching Checklist

Self-awareness about strengths and development opportunities

❑ Assessment feedback (360 instrument, interviews, and/or other data) has been conducted and debrief is complete.

❑ How can I leverage my strengths while continuing with my development?

❑ Clear development opportunities are identified.

❑ There is a clear desire to change; I want to get better at _____.

Select a skilled coach

❑ I will consider the following coach skills and qualities: listens, communicates directly, honest, articulate, trustworthy, observer of me, focused on me, perceptive, positive, discreet, experienced in group dynamics, measures progress, professional, clever, and manages his or her ego.

❑ I have reviewed bios of 1–3 coaches and have interviewed 1–2 coaches.

❑ I have selected a coach. We have discussed his/her skills, experience, and the coaching process. We talked about the coaching relationship, trust, and confidentiality.

❑ We (leader and coach) have discussed expectations related to the coaching engagement.

❑ We (leader and coach) have contracted to work together for ___ months.

Clarify your development focus

❑ I have shared assessment results, leadership strengths and development needs, and work history with my coach.

❑ My development focus will be ____; so that my work is important to my leadership and to the business, and valuable to my work group or team.

❑ I have discussed my development focus with my boss.

❑ The outcomes of my development will be _____.

Commit to change

❑ My coach and I have agreed on the frequency of coaching sessions.

❑ I have identified time for face-to-face coaching sessions, follow-up activities, and practice.

❑ I have scheduled meeting time with my coach.

❑ I have scheduled monthly meetings with my boss to review my progress.

❑ I am ready to listen and try new behaviors.

Follow a coaching process

❑ I understand the coaching process and am ready to move forward.

❑ We have written a development plan or contract that describes expected outcomes.

Manage your coaching engagement

❑ My coach has had an orientation to my organization and its culture, and knows the names of my direct reports, peers, and boss.

❑ We have discussed the best way for my coach to reach me (assistant, phone, e-mail, etc.).

❑ I have a plan to communicate with HR / Leadership development / my boss.

A checklist such as this one should be shared with organization leaders prior to beginning a coaching program.

Prepare the Boss for Coaching

One important, but not always consistent, component of a successful coaching assignment is the role of the executive's boss. The leader's direct manager (and often that manager's boss) must not only support the coaching process, but also know their responsibilities in the engagement.

Most successful assignments we have witnessed identified the boss's support as an important factor. As one leader explained, "My manager is very supportive and does an excellent job taking the time to provide feedback on coaching. He sets the tone that this is important." This leader went on to tell us that his boss made it clear that "if you need to take time out from your workday to focus on this, you have my permission to do that." Another leader concurs: "[Coaching] also has to be something that you and your boss are doing together; it can't just be something you are doing just to check it off your list."

Several poorly rated assignments often included a disinterested boss. During one interview, we asked a leader, "Was your boss aware of the coaching? Was he or she involved in any way?" The leader replied, "No—not involved, not aware, probably doesn't care." In another interview, a leader felt that his boss recommended coaching enthusiastically, but then never followed up at all after the assignment was underway. He felt it was just a *check-the-box* exercise.

We investigated the role of the boss in coaching assignments. Interestingly, organizations and coaches had much higher expectations for the boss than did leaders (Fig. 9). Twenty-four percent of leaders *don't have any expectations* for their manager, compared to ten percent of organizations. Just 23 percent of leaders felt that the *manager needs to be actively involved in [the] assignment underway*—a stark contrast to the opinion of 65 percent of organizations and 53 percent of coaches.

One successful tip is to inform the boss that he or she is the *sponsor* of the coaching assignment. Use of this wording alone automatically implies a greater role and responsibility in the coaching.

The following should be the sponsor's responsibilities:

- Inform the leader that he or she will engage in coaching.
- Be available to speak with the coach at the assignment's start, and periodically thereafter.
- Review and enhance the coaching action plan when ready.
- Provide regular feedback to the leader and coach on observed progress.
- Participate in a closing review meeting to evaluate results.

Figure 9. Role of the boss in coaching assignments—organization, leader, and coach perspectives (select all that apply).

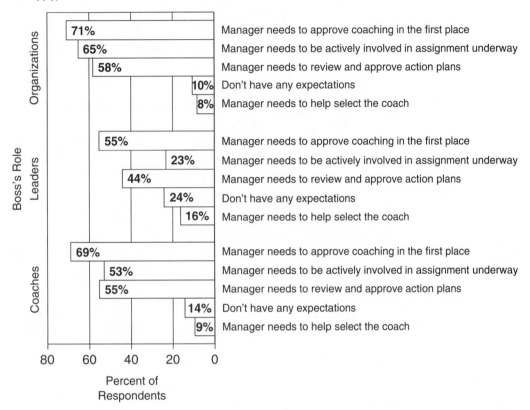

Given the significance of matching, as discussed in the following section, we prefer that bosses not play a role in the interviewing and selection of candidate coaches. Allow the leader to make this decision independently. An orientation, guide, or communication piece clarifying the role of the boss is also advised.

Don't Underestimate Matching

Leaders told us that the match to their coach was one of the most important pieces of the process, if not *the* most important—especially for longer-term assignments. For years, we've appreciated the importance of matching; and the research greatly reinforced that viewpoint.

Good matches solidly engage the leader in the trusted coaching relationship. The leader is more willing to be open, take risks, and follow the coach's recommendations.

An effective matching process also reduces the incidence of dissatisfied and disengaged leaders. Several years ago, we were asked to assign coaches to more than 30 leaders in a coaching program. We learned of two obvious coach-to-leader mismatches along the way. Later, in another division of same company, we encouraged leaders to interview and select a coach from tailored recommendations. There were no mismatches among the next 60 or more participants. Leaders are less likely to blame a failed coaching assignment on the coach if *they* picked the coach.

The two most common matching practices involve human resources or leadership development assistance. HR or LD can either match the leader with a coach or provide two or three recommended coach bios and encourage the leader to interview those coaches. Said one leader, "I looked at the top three, [HR recommendations] and for me, it was really the personal connection; I wanted to make sure that I felt I would have a good relationship with them."

Both organizations and leaders agreed that the most common matching process is for leadership development or human resources to make an *educated match*. Slightly less common is *the leader self-selects from a list of options*. This is in contrast to coaches, who believe leaders are selecting them from a list of options, followed by the *educated matching*. Some leaders told us that they selected a coach already being used by their boss or a trusted colleague.

Though the personal fit and chemistry need to be right, many leaders acknowledge the value of selecting coaches who will purposefully challenge them, rather than selecting a mirror image. One leader's advice is to "Make sure the chemistry is right, and don't waste time. It shouldn't be a chore to relate to your coach. If it is, stop, reset, and pick another." One organizational representative says, "I ask people to choose someone different from themselves."

One leader describes this balance well: "You could argue that if you feel a little bit challenged [with the coach] or a little inhibited, it might be good at keeping you on your toes." Another warns that "if the chemistry is wrong and you just don't enjoy the person, I don't think there is going to be a whole lot of productive outcome."

Some organizations are becoming more purposeful about the coaches they recommend for different leaders, characterizing their coaches according to specialty, experience, etc. One company told us that they "don't believe that all coaches are equally skilled in all areas and with all types of executives. We try to identify their respective area of expertise."

Generally, best practice companies prescreen coach bios, provide two or three options to a leader, and ask the leader to interview and select the right match.

Providing organizational leaders with a guide to selecting a coach is also helpful. Figure 10 is one such example.

Figure 10.   Guide for leaders.

Selecting the Right Coach

The most effective coaching experience begins with a good match between the executive's needs and preferences and the experience, skills and style of the coach. All coaches in our Executive Coaching cadre have been selected based on 1) key criteria and 2) interviews by our personnel. Therefore, the most important factor for you in selecting your coach is to choose one whose experience best meets your development objectives and with whom you feel you will work the best.

Our Coach Key Criteria	Our Coach Selection Criteria
• 10+ years Business Experience • 5+ years Coaching Experience • Advanced Degree • Leadership Behavior Coaching • Industry Experience a Plus • Functional Experience a Plus	• Coaching Skill & Experience • Command/Listening Skills • Ability to Establish Rapport • Fit with our Culture • Ability to Push Back • Ability to Synthesize Information • Ability to Provide Insight

Get Prepared
Prior to conducting a phone interview with potential coaches, consider which areas you would like to develop. Look through past performance reviews, culture survey data, 360 feedback, and informal manager input. This will be helpful in determining the best coach to help you.

Telephone Interview
We recommend that you review the background outlines provided and conduct a 15 to 20 minute telephone interview with the coaches of interest. Contact information is on their bios.

Consider asking:
- "Tell me about your background, and how you came to be a coach."
- "What areas of development are your specialties? What is your *strike zone*?"
- "I may want to improve in [area of development]. Tell me more about your experience coaching leaders with a similar area for development. What was your approach, and your timeframe for change?"
- "How would you describe your style? Direct? Soft? In between?"
- "How do we interact during an engagement, and with what frequency?"

Evaluate:
- Credibility as a resource
- Ability to quickly establish rapport
- Ability to maintain confidential information appropriately
- Commitment to your sustainable development and avoiding dependency on the coach

Making a Choice:
Coaches understand you're working for the *best fit* and will not be offended if you do not select them. Coaches will want to know more about your developmental goals and your level of commitment to this process. A coach may recommend an alternate coach with greater expertise in your specific developmental goal area.

Once you have made your selection, inform your new coach or the contact from whom you received the coach bios.

> If you need further guidance or want more coach choices, contact
> Jim Sample, Senior Manager, Global Talent & Leadership, 5-3075

At another organization, coaches are listed on the Web site by specific competency specialties, based on the organization's leadership model. When assignments come in, human resources identifies three coaches. Each of them has specific experience with the development issues, the leader's executive level, and often with the employee's function or business.

In Figure 11, we present a process for making an effective match of a coach to the leader. While this 5-step process considers that Human Resources or Leadership Development assists in choosing a coach, it can be adapted if pre-screening does not occur.

Some organization practitioners have indicated an interest in enhancing matching through coach/leader personality testing. One example is using Myers-Briggs (MBTI) types to create the match. We aren't certain how this might work in practice, or even whether to match similar types or opposite types. With coachees, when the organization is familiar with the MBTI, we do share our *type* (or whatever tool we're using) to better illustrate how the similarities and differences may play out over the course of the engagement.

Matching Concerns

Should a coach working with a boss be considered a candidate for the boss's direct report? On the one hand, having a common coach means he or she can learn a particular portion of the organization better, increasing their effectiveness throughout. However, this may be seen as less secure in terms of confidentiality, even though coaches maintain strict confidentiality standards. Unless there are very challenging dynamics in the reporting relationship, we still believe that an optimal leader-to-coach match overrides this particular concern.

Another caution is the incredibly satisfied executive coachee who excitedly requests his or her coach to work with all members of his or her team. The coachee may feel that the coaching experience was so life-transforming that everyone else should have the exact same experience. Organizations may accommodate this request, bypassing their normal leader qualification and coach matching processes to make it happen. Team members may feel pressure to engage in coaching with the boss's coach, unless it is truly a team coaching experience.

Again, the quality match should prevail here. Educate those sponsoring leaders on the benefits of matching and reinforce the point that the quality match should override the desire to use the same coach with everyone. Remind the coachee that coaching is a unique one-to-one relationship, and it is not possible to guarantee an identical experience for all who engage. The leader will appreciate this informed advice and will likely agree.

Figure 11. 5-step process for making an effective match.

Steps to an Effective Match

The leader/coach match is one of the most important factors in a successful coaching engagement. Follow these steps to maximize the chances for a great match:

Step 1:
Prescreen coaches according to organization criteria ahead of time. Understand each coach's background, style and areas of specialty.

Step 2:
Learn about the leader's role, background, development objectives and preferences in a coach.

Step 3:
Nominate 2–4 coaches who may best match to the leader. Consider coaches with similar backgrounds to the leader and coaches specializing in the leader's development objectives. Also consider how the style of each coach will match to the leader's (e.g., Hard charging executives respect coaches that match their style).

Step 4:
Request leader to interview some or all coaches and select the best option. Offer the leader a guide to assist in this process (see Figure 10).

Step 5:
Check leader satisfaction within 3–4 weeks of engagement start.

Watch for Stalls

In a new assignment, the most common stall point is waiting for the leader to interview and select a coach after bios have been provided. The initial energy and momentum are paused—sometimes for much too long—while everyone waits for the leader to conduct the interviews. This delay can be telling of the leader's commitment to coaching, and should be addressed.

Our solution is to notify executives that their coach recommendations are valid for only two weeks. After that we can't guarantee availability of those particular coaches. Leaders may also be told that the recommended coaches will contact them to set up the interview, rather than vice versa. Many stalled assignments can be jump-started by the coach reaching out to the leader.

Find Mismatches and Fix Them Quickly

We met a general manager from a sponsoring company who spoke to us about his coaching experience. He didn't feel that he had the right coach for him. But he didn't know he had options to do anything about it, so he continued half-heartedly through his assignment. In retrospect, he wishes he had been more assertive about changing coaches.

When preparing leaders for coaching, let them know they are entitled to switch coaches if necessary. Follow-up with each assignment approximately three to four weeks after the start to verify leader satisfaction. Consider an online coach satisfaction survey to gauge satisfaction (*see* Chapter 8). Doing this early on allows for beginning again with a new coach, generally with minimal financial impact to the organization or affected coaches.

Don't assume that leaders will automatically signal a mismatch, especially in less confrontational corporate cultures. Although coaches generally request ongoing feedback from their leaders, we cannot assume that they will get the full story. The organization should independently check on the connection.

Get Clear on Length and Frequency

How long does coaching generally last? The most common coaching duration is 6 to 12 months. Nearly three-quarters of organizations said most of their coaching assignments last between 6 to 12 months. The vast majority of coaches (86 percent) agreed with this assignment duration.

An interesting trend is apparent from the data. Coaches believe that their assignments are lasting longer than organizations do. In fact, nearly 29 percent of coaches identify assignments lasting longer than 18 months, which was not supported by any organizational respondents!

We find that coaches often work well beyond the scheduled stop period and therefore consider the assignment to be continuing in one form or another (*see* Chapter 11). Organizational participants may view the assignment as ending *officially* at a particular point in time and consider continuation to be something other than coaching.

Many organizations believe that assignments should be relatively short (up to 12 months) and focused on specific, actionable behaviors. Others perceive coaching as a longer-term, deeper, developmental intervention. One leader who received more than 18 months of coaching told us, "What I have learned from this and my experience is very, very positive. We did not follow a traditional model. I know it was expensive, but the depth that I got out of it was incredible. So I am concerned about the kind of *drive-by* model."

It is fair to say that leaders were generally less concerned about assignment length than were organizations.

We believe that leadership behavioral change generally requires 12 to 18 months to fully take effect. However, a strong start can accelerate the results of the coaching, with major behavioral changes enacted in six months. In 12 months, key stakeholders should have definitely accepted the changed behavior. After this point, the behavior is likely to be fully integrated into the leader's daily repertoire.

Several companies offered to share the way they generally approach coaching engagements. In this first example, Wal-Mart illustrates their approach to coaching lengths, allowing for longer engagements in a *lite* way.

Coaching Lite: the Wal-Mart Way

Heidi Glickman &
Margaret Durr
Wal-Mart

Wal-Mart's executive development and coaching program began in 1998. The initiative started with the executive committee, and has expanded to include coaching work with SVPs, VPs, and high-potential directors.

As a retailer working on low margins, our investment in coaching is reviewed through a budget process to ensure that it continues to add value. Given our cost-conscious culture, our coaching program has been described as *Coaching Lite* by external colleagues. The program is intensive initially, consisting of assessments, feedback from a coach, and development planning in partnership with supervisors and coaches. Because a significant investment is made on the front end, follow-up coaching sessions are less frequent, with leaders meeting or talking with their coaches usually once a quarter thereafter. The leader's supervisor also plays a considerable role in terms of having input into the process, sharing his or her perspective and holding the leader accountable for achieving their developmental goals.

The number of coaching engagements in a single period of time varies, but there are approximately 600 leaders who participate in this coaching program each year, with varying degrees of intensity. Approximately 150 leaders begin the program each year, but in any given year there is an overlap of people who are at different stages. On average, the process takes a year and a half.

Although the program focuses on accelerating development, it also aligns closely with our succession planning process. We actively plan development in order to accelerate people's readiness either to take on specific roles or to develop specific skill sets. Additionally, we provide opportunities for high potentials and up-and-coming talent to leverage this resource. In recent years, we have expanded the coaching program to be used for specific transitions, such as expatriate assignments and new executive on-boarding. In these cases, the timeframe for coaching sessions is intensified.

Reaching the APEX: How Agilent Leaders Benefit from Tiered Options for the Duration of Coaching

Christine Landon & Alison Hu
Agilent Technologies

Another example comes from Agilent Technologies, which has a well-developed approach and coaching program. The APEX program clearly defines the different lengths of each type of assignment.

Prior to designing a corporate-wide initiative, we found coaches working under all types of agreements with our leaders—some on retainer and others hourly, daily, or yearly. We believed we should standardize and simplify our offerings at Agilent Technologies, and be very thoughtful about the lengths of coaching assignments we offered executives.

We sought lengths sufficient to reinforce behavioral change, yet which also allow for introductory *get your feet wet* experiences for those more skeptical of executive coaching programs. Our program included a *results guarantee*: Executives must improve or the company wouldn't be charged for the coaching services.

APEX (Accelerated Performance for Executives) was established at Agilent in 2000, and offers three primary coaching options for leaders:

- **Base Camp.** An entry-level program; includes a 360 survey plus a two- to four-hour face-to-face coaching session.
- **Camp 2/Camp 3.** Includes a 360 survey or coach interviews, six months of coaching,* and a mini-survey.
- **High Camp / Summit.** Includes a 360 survey or coach interviews, 12 months of coaching,* and two mini-surveys.

*Coaching includes a combination of in-person and face-to-face coaching, with a *results guarantee*.

At each level leaders have the option to upgrade to a higher level of the program. To date, nearly every Base Camp leader has upgraded to High Camp or Summit after the session. Each option is priced as a flat-rate program to simplify budgeting.

To date, 100 leaders have participated in the APEX program, with more than 95 percent of them demonstrating improvement.

Next, an executive coach who also assisted as a researcher, Carol Braddick, offers a framework for thinking about the coaching engagement.

Thoughts on Duration

Carol Braddick
Graham Braddick Partnership
Study Researcher

Our prediction that standard coaching engagements will become more uniform is based on observation of the recent shift across the spectrum below:

WILD WILD WEST	*FRAMEWORK*	*UNIFORM PACKAGE*
Unknown number of coaches working on engagements of unknown length and wide ranging purposes.	Engagements that meet basic requirements: engagement objectives, sponsor, general guidelines for timeframe.	Predefined number of hours of coaching; specified hours for other activities, e.g., stakeholder interviews.

The companies participating in this study are already managing coaching in the middle and far right of this spectrum—in other words, using frameworks and uniform packages. Despite their having exited the Wild Wild West phase, we still found differences among the views of organizations, coaches, and executives on the duration of typical engagements.

Our study group was more curious about than troubled by these findings—for example, that coaches tend to report longer engagements. Coaches have offered a few explanations for the disparity in responses:

- Coaches and executives stay in touch informally following a formal wrap-up;
- Coaches perceive this follow-on period as a natural part of the relationship, including it in the perceived length of the engagement;
- Executives take a more black-and-white view—if they no longer have two-hour sessions booked, the engagement has concluded;
- Many coaches and executives contract for a second engagement that may be less intensive or event-driven—for example, a change in role.

This second engagement could be our next Wild Wild West. But we go into this potential sequel to Wild Wild West with a great base of experience with coaching. We can also take a *good news* (e.g., the executive values an external challenge) versus *problem* (e.g., an unhealthy dependency on the coach) orientation to the next phase of coaching. If a leader completes the first engagement with a greater appetite for development and reflection, that's good news, no? Our challenge is to reshape the coaching team to make best use of all resources—the executive, internal coaches, and external coaching—for the second round. If Wild Wild West has a sequel, it's likely to be thoughtfully tame.

Face-to-face or Telephone Coaching?

Is face-to-face or telephone coaching more preferable?

Most coaching is handled in person, according to approximately two-thirds of both organizations and coaches. Leaders saw things differently—only a little more than half selected face-to-face. In turn, leaders estimated a greater frequency of telephone use than coaches or organizations did. E-mail and online options were used even less.

We are speculating that leaders' responses which favored the more virtual or technology options may indicate a leader preference, rather than the reality. Leaders generally perceive coaching as something they fit into their busy schedules, so electronic support may make more sense for them.

There isn't one simple answer to the question of how best to conduct coaching. Instead, there are multiple factors to consider based on the circumstances. Five factors favor more face-to-face coaching in the mixture:

- Organizational cultures that favor face-to-face interaction (hint: very few telecommuters is a sign of such a culture);
- Global cultures that favor face-to-face interaction (Latin America, Asia, etc.);
- A senior leader for whom travel expenses are not an issue;

- Development objectives that require observational coaching (e.g., presentation skills, inspiring a team);
- An executive who takes longer to connect with unfamiliar people.

Six factors favor a mixture that includes more telephone coaching:

- Fewer coaches available near executive locations;
- Specific coaching as an add-on to training programs;
- Leaders on the road regularly;
- Leaders with a tendency to cancel or change appointments at the last minute;
- Budget limits on travel expenses;
- More frequent coaching sessions.

Regarding culture differences, one leader told us, "My coach is in another country, and I think it is more difficult to build a real relationship with trust. I would prefer to see my coach more often. We try to talk often on the phone, but it is not the same thing."

We view e-mail or online coaching as an enhancement to face-to-face and/or telephone coaching, and not as a stand-alone offer.

We find that even one face-to-face session greatly builds rapport building, which enhances future telephone sessions. Most organizations request a typical mixture (e.g., two face-to-face sessions, with the remainder by phone), but allow the leader and coach to determine what works best for them.

How frequently do coaching sessions occur? According to the Web survey, monthly sessions are most common, yet that depends on who is asked. As Figure 12 shows, coaches believe that more coaching is occurring at more frequent intervals than do organizations or leaders.

We suggest a coaching frequency of every one to two weeks, with interactions of shorter duration being preferable, even if on the phone. For example, weekly 30-minute calls are preferable to a single four-hour visit per month. A key coaching benefit is the regular, ongoing reinforcement of learning concepts; greater frequency allows for this. We usually set up a recurring weekly check-in with our leaders, with the understanding that changing schedules may require some flexibility.

Activities in Coaching

We looked at the most common activities in coaching assignments. Some activities are common to all assignments, and others are considered as options.

Leaders and coaches gave conflicting views on what activities occurred in their assignments (Fig. 13). Among our eight choices, leaders and coaches selected *action plan generation* as the top choice. *Assessment tools* was the next most frequently selected activity (69% leaders, 86% coaches). Assessment tools are covered in more detail in Chapter 5.

Figure 12.   Frequency of coaching interactions—organization, leader and coach perspectives.

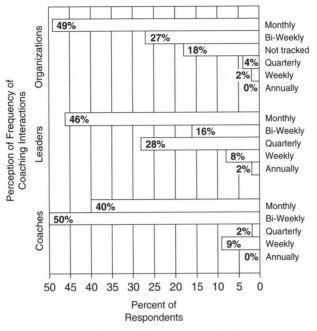

Percent of
Respondents

Figure 13.   Activities during coaching assignments—leader and coach perspectives (select all that apply).

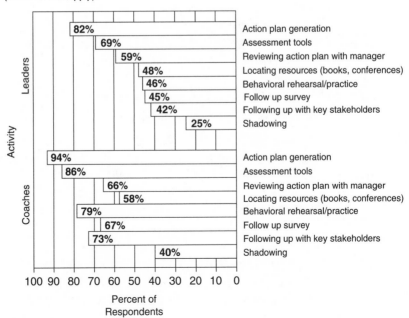

Percent of
Respondents

Responses from leaders and coaches then differ. Leaders next selected *reviewing action plan with manager* (59%) and using their coach for *locating resources (related books, conferences, trainings, etc.)* to support their change efforts (48%).

Coaches, on the other hand, next selected *behavioral rehearsal/practice* (79%) and *following up with key stakeholders* (73%). The largest leader-versus-coach perception gaps occurred for *behavioral rehearsal/practice* (a 33% difference) and *following up with key stakeholders* (a gap of 31%). On most Web survey *select all that apply* questions, leaders selected fewer activities than coaches did, with a median gap of 16 percentage points on this specific question.

Why did leaders and coaches differ so greatly in their selection of these activities? Leaders may be underestimating *behavioral rehearsal/practice* and *following up with key stakeholders* because they are less comfortable with these options. Discussing an action plan with a manager or asking a coach to locate various resources may be easier to discuss because they seem less personal.

Action Plan Generation

Most coaching assignments include an action plan that is jointly created by the leader and the coach. Action plans will include some of the following components:

- Clearly defined development objectives;
- Specific steps to achieve the development goals;
- Timelines;
- Resources required to accomplish objectives (e.g., specific training, manager's support);
- Barriers that would impede progress;
- Ways to overcome these barriers;
- Metrics to measure improvement;
- Key stakeholders to involve in development objectives.

The plan should be reviewed with the leader's manager, HR, and leadership development—either with or without the coach in attendance. The manager can confirm the development objectives and offer recommended action steps. This also increases the buy-in from the manager related to how the coaching is progressing. Following up with key stakeholders (as discussed later in this section) will uncover more action steps for the plan.

The plan should be revisited periodically. A simplified version can be laminated on a small card for portability (such as next to the leader's key card identification).

Leaders are better at remembering just a few key actions from their plans. Therefore, we recommend prioritizing the actions by greatest impact. Leaders should select the two or three actions with the highest payoff and commit to practicing them daily.

One example is a leader with poor listening skills who had a terrible habit of interrupting people. We asked her to focus only on this interrupting problem for the first few weeks. Just this one step made a major difference in her listening skills.

Our interviews suggest that organizations believe action plans are more robust and detailed than leaders, and sometimes coaches, do. If this is a concern to your program, supply coaches with an exemplary plan as an example.

A few pioneering organizations are publishing plans in an online forum to better track development objectives and progress throughout their leadership population. Leaders with similar development objectives can connect and support each other.

Behavioral Rehearsal/Practice

Behavioral rehearsal/practice is actually the role-playing of specific desired behaviors during the coaching sessions. For example, a leader seeking to be more open to others' ideas would practice responding more positively to ideas proposed by the coach. Many times we've practiced with executives on how to deliver performance feedback.

There is a large difference between conceptualizing what to say or do with others and actually practicing the right actions. Fast-moving executives will understand the concepts quickly, then want to move on to something else. Coaches should instead encourage the leader to take the extra few minutes to practice the new behavior. It is amazing how many times the executive stumbles on the first few attempts during practice. It is usually easier to *understand* new behaviors than it is to actually change. Getting leaders to practice ahead of time means that they will be better prepared to try the new behavior in front of their boss, peers, and subordinates.

Some coaches use videotape feedback as a way to highlight the leader's behavior. If available, this is a method of learning that makes a significant impact.

Following Up with Key Stakeholders

Following up with key stakeholders is a proven technique by which leaders receive ongoing input regarding their specific areas for development. Key stakeholders include managers, direct reports, peers, customers, HR, leadership development, and vendors.

Research has repeatedly proven that the more regularly leaders follow up, the more likely they will be seen as having improved in follow-up mini-surveys.

In one study by Goldsmith & Morgan[1] of more than 86,000 raters, the evidence was very clear. Leaders who discussed their development objectives regularly with others improved significantly more than those who did not. This held true no matter what type of coaching they received. Some had face-to-face interactions; others were by telephone only. Some worked with internal coaches, and others with external coaches. Some went to five-day training programs, whereas others attended no programs. This also held true across countries as well.

Following up with key stakeholders should be a nonnegotiable expectation of leadership coaching.

Leaders are encouraged to have quick, five minute individual conversations with all their key stakeholders every one or two months during coaching. The leader simply reviews what he or she is working to develop in, and then asks for any suggestions to improve in those areas. This makes key stakeholders aware of the leader's development efforts and more likely to actually notice development improvements.

We maintain a follow-up grid with every assignment. By checking off each follow-up date, we can easily see if a particular stakeholder has not been contacted in a while. Leaders don't always buy into this approach initially, because it leaves them somewhat vulnerable. But most get used to it quickly and soon accept the idea.

If a leader is slow to follow up with stakeholders, a good coach will help make it happen. In one typical example, we returned to our leader every week to find that he still hadn't begun his first round of follow-up. His reason was, "It's been busy; I haven't had a chance yet." After the third visit with no action, we said, "Well, we're scheduled to spend the next two hours together anyway. Let's get up and start visiting people." Over the next 30 minutes we visited his stakeholders and were able to have quick follow-up conversations with most of them. He called the rest on a speakerphone and e-mailed two more overseas that we couldn't get live. After we facilitated that first round, future rounds were much easier for him.

Another leader's assistant scheduled 15-minute meetings with every rater, one after another, in a conference room. We spent half a day there while he met with everyone in succession.

In both examples, the leaders accomplished three objectives. First, the stakeholders were notified of the leader's objectives. Second, the leader learned how easy follow-up can be in completing this part of the assignment. Finally, the leader got a close-up look at what the coaching would be like, and at the coach's expectations and practices.

Shadowing

Although *shadowing* is used in only about a quarter of assignments, leaders who experienced this method spoke very highly of the practice. Many interviews pointed to the incredible learning produced by this form of *observational coaching*, in which the coach has the opportunity to witness the leader in everyday activities. In particular, observational coaching is well suited to observing the leader's communication skills, meeting interactions, and presentation ability.

We worked with a research and development leader who needed help being more inspirational to his extended team of more than 40 engineers. We'd fly up and meet him 30 minutes before each team meeting, observe from the back of the room during the meeting, and then debrief him afterward. Each time, we could highlight a number of both obvious and subtle behaviors he could improve before his next meeting.

The meetings were dull status updates. We noticed that he would speak too quietly, make little eye contact, and stand behind the podium, revealing little about himself personally. We were able to get him to engage more with the audience, tell more stories from his experience, raise his voice and increase eye contact, and even provide food to relax the mood. He created more opportunities for everyone to be part of the shared vision, getting more team members to buy into it and tying everything back to the overarching goal.

We doubt that we could have understood his old behaviors as thoroughly without actually seeing them firsthand. After just one meeting using this approach, he asked us to return to every future meeting.

Although observational coaching is an effective method of providing coaching feedback, it requires more time on the part of the coach. Consequently, companies should be aware of the higher cost of this coaching technique.

Daily Metrics

Nearly all of our assignments now include daily metrics. We ask the leader to measure himself or herself on two or three key action step drivers related to the development plan and record those metrics every day. We review the latest results during each coaching session.

Here are a few examples of daily metrics:

- A leader working on listening skills gave himself a daily listening score on a 1-to-10 scale. His wife would offer her score as well.
- An executive seeking to broaden her network recorded how many contacts she made in a day, and the quality of those contacts, on a 1-to-5 scale.

- A program manager who was challenged by delegation tracked how many items he delegated each day.
- A leader wanting to improve time management kept score of how often she was late to meetings or calls.
- Another struggling listener counted—a minimum of three times a day—the number of times he first rephrased others' statements. He would e-mail us the answer every night.

Recording the metric needs to be a simple process. Keep count on a pad next to the computer, in a mobile device, on spreadsheet software, or with the help of an assistant. Results can be e-mailed, faxed, or otherwise communicated to the coach weekly.

As the adage goes, *what gets measured gets done*. Daily metrics are a simple technique to greatly enhance coaching effectiveness.

Know the Costs, but That's Not All

Ask any coach about his or her pricing, and the usual answer is *it depends*. Coach fees vary widely based on the position level of the leader; the type of coaching request; the prestige factor of the client company; the coach's availability, background, and experience; the assignment's travel requirements, and other factors. Researching these factors is helpful to unravel the mystery surrounding fees in the coaching industry.

Companies indicate that costs for coaching are high—but worth it. The two most common fee structures are by the hour or for the entire assignment. Hourly fees generally range from $300 to $500, whereas assignment fees average $15,000 for a six-month assignment and $22,500 for a one-year assignment, according to the research. Our experience generally shows industry fees higher than these, however—approximately $20,000 for a six-month assignment or $30,000 for one year. We believe that the difference is likely due either to individual coach fees or to vendors negotiating larger contracts, thereby reducing average fees.

These numbers have an incredible range, too. Some name-brand coaches may charge up to $250,000 for a one-year assignment.

Given that there were fewer international participants in the study, less pricing data was gathered internationally. Although developing markets such as Brazil, India, and China could price lower, there are fewer quality coaches available in those areas. Higher-quality coaches are quite busy, so their price isn't necessarily reduced.

Organizational interviewees expect to be more selective about how they would spend their coaching money in the future. However, the research also found that a majority of organizations do not expect coaching fees to decrease over the next few years.

Thirteen percent of leaders financed coaching out of their own budgets, and another 25 percent funded it through their managers' budgets. Most respondents—48 percent of organizations—pay for coaching out of a central leadership development budget. One company explained, "For us, starting out with a centralized payment structure gives us more of a chance to get coaching started." Yet another organization said, "We charge coaching back to them . . . we think it's important for the divisions to have ownership in developing their people and to make sure that they are sending the right people through these processes."

Some coaches and coaching vendors are offering results-guaranteed coaching, wherein coaching compensation is based on the leader's improvement on follow-up surveys. In this unique arrangement, payment is delayed and contingent upon the leader improving in the eyes of key stakeholders. In this way, an organization is paying for *results*, not activities or time spent.

Finally, with all the focus on coaching expenses, leaders rated *cost* last among factors involved in selecting a coach, whereas organizations rated *cost* third of the six factors. This indicates that the ultimate customer in this process—the leader—is clearly less price-sensitive than those working to serve that customer. Perhaps it is because the value of coaching is evaluated by more than monetary cost. One leader summed up the value of coaching well, "I don't think I'll ever have the same perspective on my career after working with [my coach]."

This chapter offers important information that serves as a benchmark for evaluating common practices in the coaching field. Although there are always things to learn from other organizations, we suggest filtering the information and suggestions through your company's unique needs when designing a program.

Coaching Highlights

This chapter offers important information to help you manage coaching engagements more effectively. Wal-Mart and Agilent Technologies shared the structure of their coaching programs. Although there are aspects to learn from other organizations, as always, we suggest filtering the information and suggestions through your company's unique needs when designing a program.

- **Get prepared.** Corporate staff should spend time with the leader to clarify coaching expectations. Name the coachee's boss as the *sponsor* of the assignment, and make sure that all participants clearly understand their responsibilities.
- **Play matchmaker.** Always allow leaders the opportunity to select their coaches, generally from a starting point of two or three coach recommendations. Check in on new assignments early to spot and correct mismatches.

- **Let it go.** Allow leaders and coaches to determine the appropriate mixture of face-to-face, telephone, and online coaching, according to the organization's culture, coaching frequency, travel schedules, and other demands. At least one initial, face-to-face session greatly facilitates rapport building.
- **Action oriented.** Although action plans may include many steps, leaders should prioritize the two or three action steps with the highest payoff and make a commitment to practice them daily. Leaders should measure their progress daily, as well.
- **Follow-up works.** Requiring the leader to follow up with key stakeholders regarding his or her development objectives yields proven benefits.

5 • The Toolbox: Instruments and Assessments

Prescription without diagnosis is malpractice.

This is a well-quoted medical phrase. Although making recommendations in a coaching assignment without a complete understanding of the issues may not be malpractice, it is at the least unprofessional, if not unethical.

Whether to use instruments and the types implemented will often mirror the company's values and beliefs. We find that some companies are very open to using a variety of instruments, whereas others tightly control their use or restrict it to a few.

So how is a company to know which instruments to use? Personality assessments . . . 360-degree feedback instruments . . . interviews—the list of tools available for coaching engagements seems endless. Tools range from off-the-shelf self-assessments to interviews, to proprietary surveys, to instruments requiring certification to use them. All companies—from small, privately-held businesses to multibillion-dollar conglomerates—need to decide what will work best for them.

Overwhelmingly, companies have come to accept the use of 360-degree instruments, surveys, or interviews. The idea of gathering information about a leader's performance from a combination of peers, direct reports, and supervisors is widely used.

But it wasn't always that way. Not too long ago, there was skepticism about how truthful people would be in giving feedback about the leader. There was concern with confidentiality, and even how the information might be used. But time and experience have shown that these situations can be addressed, and that the benefits outweigh the concerns.

If your company is just starting to use instruments, we suggest starting with the 360 to gain credibility, and then trying other instruments that are appropriate for individual coaching engagements. Over time, the company and leaders will develop a track record of acceptable assessments and be able to refer to real-life examples of what has worked.

Whereas some companies are open to the use of assessments beyond the 360, many more are at first uncomfortable about using the many other assessment tools available. In contrast, most leaders are genuinely enthusiastic about using a variety of tools. They recognize that valuable information can be gained from various sources and are open to the increased personal insight. Not surprisingly, perhaps, leaders like instruments because the information instruments provide is *all about them*.

We advocate the use of instruments of all kinds, provided they are specifically chosen for a particular leader's development and engagement. We don't suggest a one-size-fits-all approach, in which an organization or coach has a *favorite* tool that they always use. The bottom line is this: Organizations should look for coaches who have a variety of tools they can bring with them. The downside of not using instruments is that without good information up front, a coaching engagement can start off on shaky ground or take longer to be successful.

This is one area in which a company's internal human resources and leadership development practitioners can be a valuable resource for an external coach. They can provide information about:

- The company's strategies for people development, talent management, and succession planning;
- The culture of the company, so a coach can recommend appropriate instruments;
- Assessment tools that have worked or not worked in the past.

In this chapter we explore the assessment tools available for particular purposes and make recommendations based on our experience in the field.

Why Use Assessments?

Let's start with an example. Let's say there is a leader whose feedback from interviewees said she tends to be intolerant of others' styles. She doesn't understand why people don't think the same way she does. She has been known to lose her temper on multiple occasions.

Based on that information, the coach recommends three instruments: Myers-Briggs (to help her understand her own style and shed light on how others have different styles); an emotional intelligence tool (to help her understand how she controls her emotions); and the Thomas Concept (to help her understand her interactions with others). The leader enthusiastically completes all three. She has been struggling with these management issues for a long time, and she wants to try anything to help her be a better leader.

We administer and summarize the learnings from the 360 and other three assessments. The 360-degree feedback is important to highlight how the leader is perceived and show her how her behavior was consistently observed by her peers, direct reports, and bosses.

With information from the other assessments, the coach is able to identify her natural style and how she would likely interact with alternative styles, as well as examine how her emotional perspective influences personal relationships. If the coach had used only the 360, she would know what the improvement area is but would not have gained enough insight about her personal style.

In this case, the information from the feedback is powerful in terms of identifying the *what* of the issue, but it is not instructive on the *why* or the *how*. Data from the instruments helps connect the dots to show how the leader approaches situations, and how her style impacts interactions. In addition, the combined information helps the leader realize how dealing with different people requires different behaviors, and that she could be more successful by adapting her style. Being aware of her natural tendencies is the first part of being able to control her behavior.

Instruments also provide data in a way that makes it easier to discuss a leader's weaknesses. For one thing, the majority of tools are viewed as value-neutral. Their purpose is to facilitate understanding of a person's tendencies, personality, or leader characteristics—not to pass judgment as to *good* or *bad*.

Also, using several tools enables the coach to combine self-assessment ratings with feedback from others. This generally helps leaders to buy into what the data says more readily.

Gather Feedback

Although there are countless instrument options available for use in coaching, it is not surprising that our research revealed stakeholder interviews and 360-degree feedback (off-the-shelf or customized) to be the most commonplace (see Fig. 14 on page 69). Most organizations use interviews, more than half have their own 360 surveys, and just under half use generic 360 surveys off the shelf.

One-quarter of the organizations limit coaches to interviews or 360-degree feedback, with no additional tools used.

A blended mixture of 360-degree feedback and interviews can be very effectively used for feedback gathering. This allows for a gathering of both quantitative and qualitative information. One organization explained, "With the 360, we use it for quantitative information, but we also do phone interviews to get out more of the qualitative aspects of feedback, which tend to be incredibly rich in terms of providing individuals with specific information."

We often practice a blended approach to data gathering. We start with the 360-degree feedback review for the broad-brush, quantitative inquiry. Then, after selecting area(s) for development, we conduct selective interviews with key stakeholders and focus deeply on these areas. We learn more about the areas for development for the leader and about potential solutions to mastering them.

Expanding the Toolbox

We believe that organizations should be open to a wider range of assessments beyond 360-degree feedback, and that coaches should offer a large toolbox from which to select the appropriate instruments. In our experience, however, instruments work better when they are easy to understand and there is clear, practical application of that knowledge.

In Table 3, we describe different types of assessments, highlight their strengths or limitations, and give examples of instruments available.

Determining Instrument Policies

As mentioned, organizations vary in their support of using instrumentation for coaching engagements. Some indicate a preset list of instruments to use, whereas others allow flexibility for the coach to choose. Some organizations do not allow any instruments within an assignment.

Approximately half of the organizations we surveyed are open to coaches recommending instruments for each assignment. One organization demonstrates its flexibility well: "Different coaches use different tools depending on the issue, and I think that's a good thing. I would not want to overregulate the tools that coaches can use because I think that it's not necessary, and I think there is probably good learning there that we could benefit from."

However, many companies do have strict guidelines prohibiting the use of other leadership competency tools. Although companies allow some instrument use by coaches, they want to ensure that those instruments do not compete with their own. As one organization says, "As long as it is not competing with our battery of instruments, coaches can bring in other instruments." Another says, "We leverage existing assessment and 360 data we have on the individual and then allow the coach to recommend others."

Table 3   Types of Assessments

Type of Assessment	Description	Strengths	Limitations	Examples
360 Feedback	Provides feedback on leadership skills from multiple perspectives of people who work with the leader including peers, direct reports, and bosses	Gain information from multiple perspectives Can ask for feedback from a large number of participants Interviews offer valuable qualitative information Confidential input Quick to gather information Easy to administer follow-up 360 to see results Widely accepted	Limited to work perspective Not as much depth using an instrument as interviews could provide Tool may not ask questions about the leader's particular needs May have tendency to overrate and give positive feedback on instruments	• Company custom tool • Interviews (in-person or phone) • Off-the-shelf/ proprietary
Leadership Skills	Provides insight into specific leadership traits	Quantitative data from assessment; instruments frequently tested for reliability Many instruments available that provide interesting indexes such as stress or preferred leadership style Can choose tool for specific leaders issues Relatively inexpensive, easy to administer	Each has its own strengths and weaknesses to consider Require a knowledgeable coach to interpret results If self-scoring, subject to leader perception	• Emotional intel-ligence (Hay Group or TalentSmart) • Professional Dynametric Program (PDP) • Conflict management • Thomas-Kilmann
Personality/ Personal Style	Offers opportunity to examine personality characteristics that create self-awareness	Enhances well-rounded view of leader by including personal tendencies Wide variety of tools available for various leader needs Enables exploring personal tendencies beyond work situations	Many are self-assessment; provide one-dimensional view Many of the tools require certification or training by the coach	• Myers-Briggs (MBTI) • DISC, Extended DISC • SDI (Strength-Development Inventory) • Birkman Method • The Thomas Concept • 16 PF • FIRO-B/ Element-B • Hogan • LIFO • Insights • Enneagram

Table 3   Types of Assessments (Continued)

TYPE OF ASSESSMENT	DESCRIPTION	STRENGTHS	LIMITATIONS	EXAMPLES
Interests/Values	Allows leader to self-assess interests or values, understand behaviors	Easy to administer Relatively inexpensive	Primarily useful for leader versus company objectives Generally not tested for reliability Tests often given as series versus separately Usually requires specific certification of the tester	• PIAV • Strong Interest Inventory
Cognitive	Used primarily by psychologists or counselors, these test intelligence or clinical aspects	Provides insight into clinical issues High degree of reliability Comparative statistics generally available	May not be appropriate for business needs Require new-qualified coach/certification Strictly controlled instruments—many require permission to use	• WAIS • Clinical/psychological assessment

Our research found that after 360-degree feedback, the Myers-Briggs Type Inventory (MBTI) is the most-used instrument (Fig. 14). Thirty-seven percent of organizations have used MBTI. In addition, Emotional Intelligence tools (such as Hay Group or TalentSmart) are seeing increased use.

Although no self-report instrument scored above 16 percent usage from leaders (except MBTI), one general point to emphasize is that overall, leaders enjoy them. Says one coach, "They [leaders] love any and all tools—especially if they are new and different."

In fact, we seldom see resistance from leaders. They almost always welcome the chance to become more self-aware and learn about their preferences and styles. However, the coach should be sensitive enough to ensure that this is the case with each specific coachee. As one person advised, "I have participated in a variety of assessment tool activities in my career and find that it is most helpful when the participants understand how the 'personality' tests and 'touchy-feely' activities relate directly to their work."

Figure 14.   Instruments used—organization, leader, and coach perspectives (select all that apply).

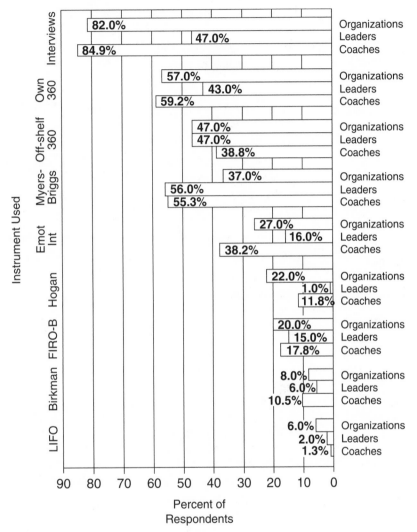

Also, leveraging instruments internationally can be a challenge. Many instruments are available only in English, which is not always usable around the world. One international coach tells us, "Most [instruments] are very U.S.-biased. I am constantly searching for more globally appropriate ones, particularly for East Asian leaders." As one organization tells us, "Even though English is the language of the company, it is foolish not to translate instruments into other languages."

There is the relatively minor issue of who should pay for the additional instruments. We generally see an equal mix of the company paying the extra cost or coaches taking it out of their fees. The cost of most instruments is under $100. We suggest that organizations provide an additional spending budget up front, with pre-approval to cover these costs. Coaches can then administer instruments at their discretion.

Coaches are advised to increase their instrument capabilities. Only 55 percent of coaches surveyed used the MBTI and 38 percent used Emotional Intelligence. Of all the other assessments, no other tool was selected by more than 20 percent of coaches. One thing organizations can do to change this situation is to request or require that coaches have a bigger toolbox. Organizations can also invite their coaches to trainings on specific tools.

How to Manage Tool Selection

Companies can enhance their coaching programs by expanding the use of instruments. Although 360-degree feedback instruments are the foundation of leader assessment, they are not enough. Other tools and assessments can provide valuable data, insight, and direction for a leader's development.

Organizations are cautioned to avoid the one-size-fits-all approach, to not overuse one instrument, and to choose coaches who offer a variety of instruments in their toolboxes.

Allow coaches the flexibility—and budget—to utilize tools they believe would add value to the engagement. However, all leadership development coaching assignments should work from the organization's leadership competency model. Insist that coaches work from your organization's model. They should not introduce their own leadership models into the engagement unless the company does not have one of its own.

Coaching is often a delicate mixture of art and science. In order to approach each assignment with care and insight, companies should be open to careful diagnosis, and coaches must be prepared to do it. Given a qualified coach, organizations would generally be wise to trust the coach's recommendation for the use of new tools—and coaches would do well to continue to add to their toolboxes.

Remember: *Prescription without diagnosis is malpractice.*

Coaching Highlights

There is a wide variety of instruments used for coaching assignments, ranging from 360-degree feedback instruments, to those focused on characteristics such as leadership or preferences, to cognitive and psychological tests. Organizations vary in regard to their acceptance and use of instruments. We advocate a general openness to using tools and encourage coaches to come equipped with a well-stocked toolbox.

- **Choose wisely.** Instruments can provide valuable information to use in a coaching assignment, provided they are specifically chosen for a particular leader's development and engagement. Avoid a one-size-fits-all approach in which the company or coach uses a *favorite* tool versus one appropriate for the engagement.
- **Start with a 360.** Start with the 360 to gain credibility, and then try other instruments. Keep track of acceptable assessments and real-life examples of what has worked.
- **Stay flexible.** Unless your company has a specific policy to the contrary, we recommend being open and flexible to using assessments of all kinds. Partner with the coach to determine what will yield the best results for your leaders.

6 • Balancing Consistency and Flexibility

Think Starbucks versus the local coffee houses.

At Starbucks, you know what you are getting. No surprises—the beverages, music, and environment are *consistent*, no matter where you are in the world. Quality is predictable. At the neighborhood coffee house, however, the experience varies. Each coffee house is unique in its own way, and whereas its quality is less predictable, it can exceed the known entity in terms of uniqueness and creativity.

Similarly, organizations struggle greatly with the consistency debate in managing their coaching programs. Should you strive to offer a consistent experience to all of your leaders across the company and around the world? Should you work to standardize instruments, processes, methodologies, result metrics, and costs?

Or should you leave coaching up to the unique combination of leader needs and coach style? Should you let leaders and coaches negotiate their own arrangements, processes, deliverables, etc.?

We've watched organizations struggle with this very dilemma—not just at the start of a new program, but from that point onward. We've seen this challenge surface in large and small organizations equally.

One of the major inspirations for our study was the concern expressed by organizations in regard to consistency. Companies were constantly struggling with how to offer—or if they *should* offer—a consistent experience to all of their leaders. Many were trying to find a happy medium as best they could.

There's good reason to consciously decide whether or not to manage coaching consistently. We would hear various horror stories of coaching run amok, such as, "What we found was that someone was still being coached. People would say, 'Do you know we are paying X dollars for a coach for Mary or John?' 'No, that was two or three managers ago.'" No one at the firm had any idea why the coach was there or what they were doing.

In another company, a leader warned us, "Coaching has to have a deliberate objective in mind, and I think mine was a little fuzzy. It's the way my company uses coaches. I thought the whole thing was kind of sloppy."

We'll take a look at consistency questions in this chapter.

Be Consistent—or Not

We asked organizations, "How important is it that a consistent process or methodology be followed in your organization's approach to coaching?" Approximately half (51%) of the organizations felt that consistency was *somewhat important* or *very important* (*see* Fig. 15, which combines the two measures).

Perhaps not surprisingly, leaders and coaches felt that consistency was *less important* than organizations did, scoring 40 percent and 41 percent, respectively. Leaders interviewed seemed unconcerned about consistency throughout the organization; they were more interested in whether coaching could work for them individually. "I think having [programs] customized to the needs of the individual is the way to go," a leader commented. "If it's too structured, too rigid, too much of a template, it would lose its value."

Figure 15.   Importance of consistency with the process—organization, leader, and coach perspectives.

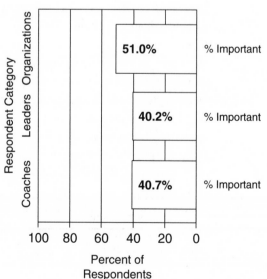

However, 37 percent of organizations felt that consistency was *somewhat unimportant* or *very unimportant*, appreciating that every engagement could be unique. We found this number to be a rather vocal minority, supporting the special one-to-one relationship of coaching and not trying to overmanage it.

Often, this desire for consistency is an organization's response to the fact that coaching outcomes are not easy to measure. When metrics are difficult to implement, there is a greater need to at least control the activities of the intervention. One coach offers clarification: "If you are doing large-scale coaching projects at a company, having a commitment that the coaches use similar or same methodology is becoming increasingly important, because these leadership development folks are really under pressure to measure the ROI impact." A leader says, "I do think, however, there is a need for some checkpoint or some evaluation, some confirmation that whatever the goals of the coaching would be, that they have been achieved."

As a government agency, the California Public Employees' Retirement System has created a program that is consistent year after year. They use a familiar 360-degree instrument, coaches, and process, and they are able to compare results over time.

Keeping Coaching Alive: Nearing a Decade of Success

Pat Santillanes & Anthony I. Lamera
California Public Employees' Retirement System (CalPERS)

CalPERS is the largest public pension fund in the United States, with more than $246 billion in assets. In 1996, it became clear that training and development (T&D) would be one of several key strategic priorities for the organization. A large-scale needs analysis drove our comprehensive T&D effort, which continues to this day.

Early on, we instituted the belief that personal leadership development was a requisite part of working at CalPERS. It is now just an accepted understanding that the 360 and the coaching process are permanent fixtures at CalPERS.

Under the leadership of Fred Buenrostro, CEO, we are now entering our fourth round of 360 feedback and executive coaching for all management and executive staff—more than 250 employees. Every one of our leaders, from first-line supervisors to the CEO, receives 360 feedback and external coaching. In each iteration, the CEO and the executive team begin the process, followed by our division chiefs, managers, and supervisors.

In the most recent round, coaching included a 360 feedback and workshop, four phone calls with an external coach over a six-month window, plus support from the Fort Hill Development Engine© online tool. Assignments concluded with a mini-survey to measure the participant's improvement over time. During each round, selected executive leaders or senior managers would also qualify for 6- or 12-month in-depth coaching assignments.

CalPERS uses a customized 360 tool that we have reused year after year, watching these scores improve with each iteration.

This commitment has been highly successful for us as an organization. Follow-up mini-survey results, coach satisfaction surveys, and anecdotal data testify to the success of this program. As a Sacramento-based public employer, we compete for valuable talent with other public sector and financial institutions. We have found that this program contributes a great deal to our goal of being a destination employer in attracting, developing, and retaining our talent.

Add Consistency to Taste

Organizations looking to increase consistency can learn from some of our surprising research findings. We found that many simple, basic methods for consistency were underutilized.

Only 55 percent of organizations check in informally with leaders regarding their coaching process. Leaders told us they would actually like more check-in from organizations regarding their engagements.

Only 35 percent of organizations require coaches to have a formal coaching plan that is reviewed or inspected, and only 27 percent of organizations ask coaches to submit written progress reports. Just 44 percent of coaches say someone internally tracks key milestones of the coaching process in the organizations that they support.

Finally—and most surprisingly—only 14 percent of coaches report being paid based on meeting key milestones (for example, partial payment on submission of the action plan and final payment after the results survey is conducted).

We suggest deciding which elements will be controlled, and what will be left alone. Each organization will have specific preferences regarding consistency. They will require the non-negotiables (e.g., standardized pricing or written action plans submitted) and will leave other aspects alone (e.g., how often coaching is conducted or what instruments are used).

As one company puts it, "We do not require coaches to follow any particular coaching model, but we do expect them to cover all the coaching touchstones we consider important." Another notes, "We have consistent processes for coaching in general, and we require a learning contract for coaching engagements. But how the coaches do the work is up to them. That is their specialty, and what they were trained to do." Another company representative commented, "I like the idea of a general framework that has a fair amount of flex built into it."

One organization is considering several levels of consistency among its various programs: "We don't have one methodology across the company—we have various levels. We would like to have a tiered approach, where we can say 'we have got this offering that accomplishes X, and it has this level of rigor and this level of cost.' We would like to get to the point of three or four service offerings that we can plug and play."

The following consistency framework will assist practitioners in determining which elements to actively control, and which to leave alone.

LOW CONSISTENCY	HIGH CONSISTENCY
INITIATE COACHING	
Anyone seeking a coach may use one	Centralized control over coach usage; requests screened for approval
MATCHING	
Leaders select the right coach for them	HR/LD assigns coaches to leaders
PROCESS	
Each assignment is unique; coach/leader to determine details	Standardized process for every coaching assignment
INSTRUMENTS	
Coaches employ any instruments they recommend	No additional instruments are permitted/approved list of instruments
REPORTING	
Assignments are not centrally managed	HR/LD checks in with leader regularly/coach submits written progress reports
OUTCOME MEASUREMENT	
Outcome metrics are determined on a case-by-case basis	Standard metric for all assignments; results aggregated corporately
COACH SCREENING	
Coaches selected at the local level	HR/LD locate and approve all coaches according to standard criteria set/one or few coaching vendors
COSTS	
Individual negotiation based on assignment specifics	Centralized cost management

Organizations interested in increasing consistency within their coaching programs can consider some of the following:

- List of prescreened coaches and/or the same vendor to help control quality and process;
- Internal coordination to manage activities;
- Screen coaching requests to ensure that coaching is the right intervention;
- Coaching Management System (project management system for coaching activities);
- Clarity on key milestones, and pay coaches based on key milestone attainment;
- Clarifying use of assessment tools;
- Formal action plan shared with others;
- Checking in with leader periodically;
- Coaches to submit written progress reports;
- Consistent metrics at the end of each assignment;
- Orientation for new coaches;
- Coach symposium and conference calls;
- Coaches to attend, or even teach, part of a leadership development program (to better know the content).

The decision on what will and will not be controlled is likely influenced by an organization's tendency toward centralization or decentralization. Manage the controlled elements well and let the others go.

At Johnson & Johnson, achieving consistency among more than 200 operating companies is quite a challenge. But as Janet Matts explains, a basic framework can be established that allows for the flexibility inherent in a decentralized organization.

Coaching Across 230 Companies: Providing a Systematic Framework, Respecting Entrepreneurial Cultures

Janet Matts
Johnson & Johnson

Johnson & Johnson is known for its decentralized organizational structure and management philosophy. We have more than 230 operating companies located in 57 countries.

Any *corporate* function or service that provides support to these individual operating companies must learn to navigate the innate tension between organizational consistency and the spirit of entrepreneurial independence. To accomplish this we must supply first-rate work in a user-friendly framework that allows each Operating Company (OpCo) to make it their own. There is no mindset better suited for this difficult challenge than *servant leadership*, which is often discussed in coaching. This is the opportunity to walk our talk.

Moreover, given the focus on continued growth and globalization, along with sensitivity to reducing costs, it has become increasingly critical to provide significant leveraged value across the organization.

We can't reasonably expect to make decisions and design processes and tools, and then see them immediately implemented everywhere. Our challenge is to create the guidelines, goals, processes, and components of coaching systems and to roll them out—making it easier for our colleagues, saving a lot of duplicative efforts, and leveraging opportunities—while providing (widespread) consistency of methodology. Each operating company can then tailor the work to meet its needs while also realizing the value that, in the past, may not have been available, or accessible before via technology and our cross-pollination efforts.

We've created a large coaching network for our business partners to tap. Coaches complete an information worksheet regarding their philosophies, work history, background, specialty areas, and where they've worked in J&J previously. We keep these worksheets in an electronic database for easy reference and referral. We have selected four international coaching partners that have resources around the world, and we have created a team of Johnson & Johnson coaches from each organization. Certain subsets of this pool are then allocated to specific programs, in addition to using a variety of high-quality boutique or independent coaches who have relationships across the Johnson & Johnson family of companies.

Although Johnson & Johnson manages consistency across many operating companies, Dell has greater consistency needs because of their more centralized structure. Dell shares how they manage their global coaching practice and how they keep track of all their coaching activities.

Behind-the-Scenes: Managing a Global Executive Coaching Practice

Kimberly Arnold & Barbara Kenny
Dell, Inc.
Stephen E. Sass
*Alliance for Strategic Leadership,
Coaching and Consulting*

A few years ago, we realized that our executive coaching network required additional oversight. We engaged the Alliance for Strategic Leadership (A4SL)/CoachSource to centralize the executive coaching process and provide an additional level of global program management support.

Our partner provides two part-time managers dedicated to Dell, who monitor and report on all executive coaching activities (e.g., new assignments, regular status reporting, billing, and special data requests). As coaches themselves, they add value through their direct coaching engagements and involvement with our senior leaders.

Our partners have helped us automate many of the coaching management processes, which has greatly reduced the time required to approve and initiate new coaching engagements.

We also work closely with internal coaching owners in each business unit to oversee assignments. We maintain an internal website for these business partners with bios of all approved coaches in the global network, sorted by geographic region and specialty area.

Most importantly, our vendor maintains a robust coaching management system to support Dell's growing coaching practice. As new requests for coaching are received from Dell, all pertinent information about the leader is automatically populated in the system, which then triggers an automated workflow and request for approval to the leadership development representative assigned to that business.

Our coaching managers then assign potential coaches to this leader based on his or her areas for development and matched against our coach locations and specialty areas. Once a coach is selected, automated e-mails inform all key stakeholders of the new engagement, providing each with the necessary information (e.g., assignment length, end date, cost information) to begin the assignment. The information also interfaces with Dell's online billing system to begin the payment process.

A satisfaction survey is run after one or two months and an impact survey is conducted at the assignment's end. Both of these surveys are semi-automated. Aggregate scores are tracked, allowing managers to review coach results individually.

In addition to daily program administration and reporting, our partners are also largely responsible for new coach sourcing. They have been instrumental in helping us increase our network in order to find and engage highly trained coaches in areas outside the United States, such as China, where that can be a challenge.

Coaching Highlights

Offering a consistent coaching experience for all leaders is a major concern for some organizations. Other firms don't try to control the process at all, letting the leader and coach work it out for themselves. This tendency toward control is often related to an organization's natural tendency toward centralization. A dispersed company such as Johnson & Johnson shows how flexibility is built into a basic framework. In contrast, Dell manages its coaching program for much greater consistency.

- **Choose what to control** and leave the rest. Factors to consider: who initiates coaching, matching, the process, instruments, reporting requirements, outcome metrics, coach screening, and costs.

- **Increase consistency, if needed.** Consistency can be increased through a company internal coordinator, a coaching management system, clarity on key milestones, standardized assessment tools, an action plan template, checking in with the leader, and consistent metrics.
- **Keep coaches connected.** Consistency can also be increased through a set pool of coaches who are oriented and connected to the company regularly, through conference calls, forums, and other venues.

7 • Bringing Coaching Internal

If imitation is the sincerest form of flattery, then the coaching field should feel honored. Companies are now trying to duplicate the effectiveness of external coaching with internal coaches, which demonstrates respect for the coaching field.

Over the past five years, organizations have increasingly desired to build a coaching expertise by employing coaches within the company. Although not for every company, an internal coaching capability has tremendous appeal in terms of reducing costs and reliance on external resources. But it is not an easy venture to undertake, and it should be approached with care.

There are two main reasons to build an internal coaching pool. The first is a desire to replicate the high impact of external executive coaching at a lower cost. Although internals (rather than external coaches) may be provided to coach executives, internals are used most often for other groups, such as first-line supervisors and mid-management. None of the companies participating in our research used internal coaches for C-level leaders.

The second reason for having internal coaches is a belief that they would be more effective, either for a specific assignment, or because of a particularly strong or unique corporate culture.

Indeed, there is great appeal to building an internal coaching community, and it can be done at any company, large or small. More important than size or type of industry, the company needs to have qualified resources, the support of executive leadership, and a *desire* to bring some of the coaching internal.

In this chapter, we provide a discussion of the pros and cons of internal coaching. In addition, we've included examples of four companies that have created successful internal programs.

Consider the Opportunity

Along with the increase in external executive coaching, our research also showed an increasing interest in internal coaches. When asked about the use of internal coaching, 57 percent of the participating organizations expect their use of internal coaches to increase, and another 40 percent plan to continue their current usage.

Internal coaches may work either full-time or as a part-time coach with other responsibilities. Almost always, internal coaches find themselves with additional responsibilities in the company, even if they are supposedly full-time coaches. About one-third of leaders we surveyed have worked with an internal coach.

What determines whether an internal or an external coach should be used for a specific assignment? Companies indicate that the most important factors are:

- The level of leader being coached;
- Leader preference for an internal coach;
- Available time from an internal coach;
- Cost considerations.

In talking to leaders, 59 percent indicated a preference for an external coach, and only 12 percent preferred an internal coach. Twenty-nine percent did not have a preference. One organization explained the decision criteria this way: "We may select internal due to the knowledge of the company ... but occasionally we go the other way to allow the person room to really explore the issues more freely." However, one leader we met was very critical, suggesting that: "Using an internal person as a coach is a lot like a dental hygienist performing oral surgery."

Compare Internal to External Coaching

There are many consistent criteria as to *what makes a successful coach* that are true of either external or internal coaches. Strong coaches focus on results, are good listeners, offer useful recommendations, and help the leader stay on track. Whether the coach is internal or external doesn't impact these qualities. So what are the benefits or differences between the two categories of coaches?

Table 4 demonstrates some of the benefits and drawbacks of using internal or external coaches.

Table 4   Benefits and Drawbacks of Internal and External Coaches

	BENEFITS	DRAWBACKS
INTERNAL COACHES	• Lower cost • More control and consistency over methods • Greater understanding of organization's culture • Additional exposure/ knowledge of leader • Scheduling flexibility • May be able to spend more time observing leaders in action	• Managing time can be challenging • Perception of less confidentiality • Perceived as less credible • Having the qualifications—not always with advanced degrees, experience, or certification as coach • Limited exposure to different organizations and best practices
EXTERNAL COACHES	• Higher credibility • Greater objectivity • Experience in many organizations, industries, and business environments • Higher level of confidentiality • Bring fresh perspective • As their main profession, dependent on being successful at every coaching assignment • Broadened variety of coaching skills • May be specialized in fields of practice • Greater exposure to other coaches and best practices in the field	• Higher cost and expenses • Less familiar with company's culture and politics • Inconsistent methods across pool of coaches • Less availability without notice

Figure 16.   Critical success factors for internal coaches—coach perspective (internal coaches only) (select all that apply).

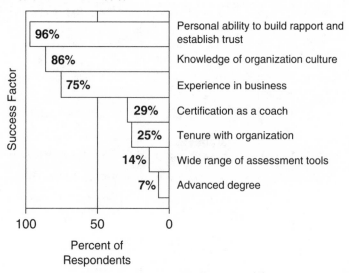

The critical factors required of a successful internal coach (as rated in our research) are presented in Fig. 16. The highest responses were for *personal ability to build rapport and establish trust, knowledge of organization culture, and experience in business.*

Two of these three top factors also match what leaders selected as most important in picking a coach: rapport and business experience (*see* Chapter 9).

The Positives of Internal Coaching

As noted above, there are many benefits to building an internal coaching pool. Although this is not an easy venture, some companies are committed to making it happen. Building an internal coaching community requires executive support, infrastructure to manage it, and a long-term commitment by the company. It is also easier if there is a track record of successful coaching.

The following narrative describes how one company, the Progressive Group of Insurance Companies, approached creating an internal coaching program.

Internals as Coaches

Elaine Roberts & Kim Deutsch

The Progressive Group of Insurance Companies

We knew we had leaders who—given the right process and tools—could effectively coach other leaders, but we lacked a singular methodology for them to use. We also knew that the program needed to integrate seamlessly within our culture.

Progressive is a unique, self-reliant organization that has focused on leveraging our people to drive company innovation and growth. Progressive people see more credibility with and respond more favorably to skills and knowledge shared with them by other Progressive people. We have a strong track record of developing and implementing programs internally, using external resources only when the subject matter expertise is not available internally.

To address these challenges, we decided to evaluate thought leaders in coaching who would be interested and willing to collaborate with us on a tailored solution. We ultimately partnered with the Alliance for Strategic Leadership.

Through a series of joint design sessions with Frank Wagner and Brian Underhill, we tailored Marshall Goldsmith's behavioral coaching process to our culture. We also incorporated specific Progressive specific case studies and developed our own version of the mini-assessment linked directly to our Leadership assessment. These design sessions resulted in a highly interactive two-day session where participants were trained in the coaching process, as seen through the lens of the Progressive culture and environment.

Approximately 30 senior human resource executives, including the chief human resource officer and her direct reports, have been trained as internal coaches. The coaches remain engaged and connected to each other after the training through peer support groups that meet to discuss challenges, successes, techniques, and experiences.

These senior human resource executives have served as coaches for other senior executives, including group presidents and company officers. These coaching assignments last approximately 12 months.

Overall, our results have been worth our investment in this process. Mini-assessment results and anecdotal evidence acknowledge improvement in our leadership competency development. Not only did our leaders' behaviors improve in the eyes of key stakeholders, but our coaches also received excellent quantitative feedback on their coaching effectiveness.

As Progressive Insurance did, Intel has developed an internal coach cadre. The following account describes how their corporate culture influenced their decision, their training of internal coaches, and the program they have today.

Internal Coaches at Intel

Lori Severson &
Dorothy Lingren
Intel Corporation

At Intel we felt that internal coaches would add value at the mid-manager levels.

In the unit supporting most of our technology and manufacturing business, the organizational development (OD) manager felt it was critical that OD talent become more solid in their abilities to coach the senior leadership team. She began investing in the training of a cadre of coaches. These coaches all received extensive external professional training with a coaching training organization.

In a similar time frame, the corporate leadership development team was benchmarking and increasing the use of external coaching and repositioning coaching as a key development tool for senior leaders.

Eventually, the business unit and corporate efforts joined forces. A pool of external coaches had already been launched to support senior leader development. We decided to make a formal offer of internal coaches targeted at middle managers across the company.

To launch a coaching offer, we pulled together the group that had received professional coaching training to consider many elements: Who to target? How to target them? How to align coaches? What are the competencies that are necessary for competent coaches? What are the necessary standards? Among other things, we agreed that our coaches needed certification from one of the major coaching schools (New Ventures West, Hudson Institute, or Newfield Network) and at least one year of coaching experience, with internal client testimonials.

We are keeping the coaching community connected with a series of ongoing meetings. This year we brought in our expanded group of external coaches for a one-day summit on business issues, along with our internal coaches as well.

Today we have a small pool of coaches that give 10 to 20 percent of their time to the larger Intel coaching offer. We have a standard working agreement, a code of conduct, and a consistent measurement.

Challenges for Internal Coaches

Of course, there are also challenges for internal coaches. One of the greatest tests an internal coach faces is the ability to achieve as much credibility as an external coach. This can be even more difficult if the internal coach previously held a different position in the company.

It seems natural to transfer a leadership development or human resources professional to become a coach, and sometimes it is. But this can be a difficult transition. Leaders often relate the potential coach to his or her prior work, remember previous interactions, or are not able to see the coach in this new role.

New coaches may also have difficulty moving away from their familiar human resources or leadership development role to the new role as a coach. Internal coaches need to build their reputation over time and prove their ability, in terms of both coaching skills and maintaining confidentiality.

In general, internal coaches remain incredibly busy. In fact, they selected *time* as their biggest challenge. Figure 17 also shows that respondents indicate other challenges, such as *concern for protection of confidentiality, too close to the situation to see clearly,* and *difficulty challenging higher management.* The last item could be considered an underestimation by some, although one coach stated, "It takes guts to challenge higher management, and it is critical to your success. You have to be willing to do it!"

Figure 17.   Greatest challenges for internal coaches—coach perspective (internal coaches only) (select all that apply).

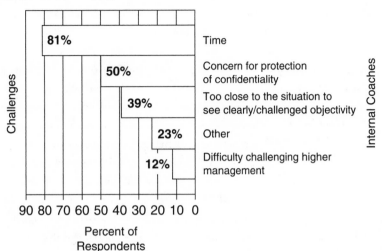

One difficulty in creating an internal coaching pool is the low availability of well-qualified internal coaches. The practice is simply too new to have a large talent pool. One option is for companies to take it upon themselves to develop their own internal coaches. But this, too, can be chancy if the leaders feel that the coaches lack experience and expertise. It is critical that the new program be credible, which can be difficult with a new internal coaching pool.

Challenges in building an internal coaching pool can be overcome in several ways. First, hire external coaches to serve as full-time internal coaches. Second, allow the new internal coaches to begin coaching in areas where they were not previously working, such as in a different division. This enables the internal coach to build a reputation in his or her new role. Finally, avoid using current human resources or leadership development staff who have other responsibilities. Internals who are *coaches first* may be perceived as more credible and better able to handle confidentiality.

Leader-as-Coach

Increasingly, organizations are becoming more interested in teaching line leaders and supervisors to be better coaches. With better coaching skills, bosses can assist employees with on-the-job situations and performance management duties.

A new generation of *leader-as-coach* training programs is now on the scene. We designed one program in which we coached recipients who, in turn, coached the next level down of direct reports.

One organization told us, "We believe . . . whether it be external coaching or internal coaching [in] developing the capability in our people to coach each other."

Bell Canada, as one example, shows us how they've strived for coaching mastery among their leaders.

Coaching Mastery at Bell Canada

Mary O'Hara
Bell Canada

At the more senior levels in the organization we deploy a program called Coaching Mastery. This program was developed to instill advanced coaching skills in key executives who would also transfer these skills to our next generation talent at the director and general manager level. One key element is the development of mastery-level conversation skills. Over the past two years, approximately 60 of our S/VP executives have benefited from this program.

The purpose of our shared learning is not to fill a gap, answer a need, or eliminate a personal weakness—nor do we review the fundamental steps and skills required to coach employees. Our challenge is beyond coaching. We seek to embrace a deeper knowledge and a higher skill set to influence others (direct reports, peers, and those more senior).

Learning Approach

1. Refine the ability to focus on business results *and* inspire the personal performance required to achieve them;
2. Develop a powerful capacity to hold the levels of attention and intention required to influence high-performing leaders;
3. Acquire mastery-level conversation skills that are beyond the competency-level tools of goal setting and asking probing questions through facilitated coaching and practice with a network of trusted colleagues.

The 12-month process includes:

- A *one-day workshop* intended to introduce the philosophy and skills of mastery. Time is given to observe, learn and practice the mastery level skills.
- Three *skills transfer workshops*, where executives meet in smaller subgroups and work in triads to anchor and refine the skills of evoking excellence in others. The sessions are videotaped and reviewed by the group.
- *Personal follow-up conversations* conducted by our Masterful Coaches, either in person or by telephone, following each skills transfer workshop. Each conversation facilitates the personal breakthroughs required to lead with integrity from a mastery-level skill set.

- A *concluding workshop* to consolidate learnings and insights and formulate our personalized ongoing development requirements.

As a result of this approach and learning journey, all leaders have expressed an increased ease and expansion of their ability to influence, both within the organization and externally.

We believe that more and more organizations will integrate a leader-as-coach concept more formally into their coaching programs. There is a lot of buzz about this in companies, and it is something every organization is able to implement.

In this next excerpt, Kenneth J. Rediker demonstrates how his company, Saudi Aramco, has raised the expectation of executives to coach and have effective conversations with employees.

Coaching within Saudi Aramco

Kenneth J. Rediker, Ph.D.
Saudi Aramco

Saudi Aramco is the world's largest producer of oil, providing this vital source of energy to all major economic regions of the world. As Saudi Aramco has come to play a more visible role in the world's energy industry, the expectations for its leaders have continued to evolve accordingly.

Coaching, as a key element of managing and developing talent, has received increased attention at Saudi Aramco since the mid-1990s. Initial formal efforts sponsored by our senior management included first steps with 360s and a very successful workshop called *Coaching for Excellence* that was designed and delivered by Dr. David Noer. Our coaching workshop used the well-recognized *Assessment, Challenge & Support* model. Feedback from our managers who attended the program suggested that this model provided a practical and focused approach for both thinking about and holding coaching sessions with employees.

However, our experience over the years with the coaching program and follow-up assessments highlighted the need to strengthen the quality of our conversation skills as a foundation for more effective coaching and performance management discussions. Although we are accustomed to successfully building multibillion-dollar oil and gas projects, building an infrastructure of leaders who are effective coaches has posed its own set of challenges. Skills to be strengthened include preparing for the coaching conversation, beginning the conversation, using questions to more effectively shape the conversation, and following up on a more regular basis to assess progress.

In recent years, with the active support of senior management, we have reemphasized the expectation that current and emerging leaders will be expected to be much more capable at engaging and developing their employees.

Thus, coaching and conversation skills, which are fundamental to managing and developing talent, continue to receive systematic attention.

Additionally, we initiated a new corporatewide performance management process in 2003 that establishes some baseline requirements in terms of ongoing communication and performance discussions between supervisors and subordinates. Although this system provides a valuable process to encourage coaching discussions and track development progress, it cannot substitute for the productive and sometimes difficult conversations that arise in a coaching relationship.

Mentoring

We feel the need for a quick clarification of the difference between mentoring and coaching. The distinction is often a bit fuzzy. In our research, we noticed that people we interviewed would sometimes describe mentoring as internal coaching, at least according to our definition.

To us, *mentoring* refers to a relationship in which someone within the company (the mentor) assists another person (the protégé). The mentor takes time to help the protégé, often by providing advice or a better understanding of the work environment, culture, office politics, or the protégé's new position; or by teaching them something specific that is useful in their job. Frequently, this is a voluntary arrangement by both parties, and they manage it without a formal process. The mentor and protégé decide when to meet, for how long, and how to work together. Each has a regular job assignment; the mentoring process is an extra activity.

There are no specific qualifications to be a mentor. Protégés choose a mentor whom they respect and view as someone who could be helpful in their career. A mentor can work with several protégés at once, and vice versa. Anyone, regardless of level, title, or performance, can have a mentor. Accordingly, mentoring often looks a lot like teaching, advice counseling, or feedback. Mentors are not paid, but in more formal programs they are recognized on performance reviews as contributing to leadership development in the company. In recent years, companies have begun to take steps to standardize mentoring programs, but they are not yet at the same formalized level as coaching programs.

In contrast, coaching is a formal arrangement between a leader and a coach. It is sponsored by and—because there is a cost involved—paid for by the company. External coaches are paid by the assignment, whereas internal coaches receive a company salary. There is almost always a formal process to be followed, such as an assessment, a written action plan, and a contracted working arrangement. Coaches are skilled professionals, and assignments are limited to selected leaders and focused on specific skill objectives. Coaching is provided only to executives or leaders who are high performers, as part of their leadership and career development.

We will not go into mentoring in detail, except to provide this clarification. We agree that mentoring programs can be helpful. They are especially positive when used to bring onboard new associates, learn about certain aspects of a job, and to enable all levels of the company to have some development opportunities. We do not see mentoring as a substitute for coaching, however.

The Debate Continues

With the rise in coaching has come a parallel rise in the use of internal coaches. We can expect to see this practice continue, especially at large companies or those that employ many external coaches.

As expected, there is controversy in regard to internal coaching. External coaches do not always welcome the trend toward internal coaching. This is partly because internal coaching is perceived to threaten their livelihood, and partly because they think that coaching is serious business. They do not want to see the field compromised by programs that are not successful. However, some external coaches have transitioned part of their practice by helping companies train internal coaches.

Our recommendation is for organizations to find a balance between internal and external coaching. The benefits are greater flexibility for the company to have a variety of coaches available, the ability to match a coach (internal or external) to a specific assignment, and the ability to manage both costs and expertise. Companies should also consider the leader-as-coach concept, in addition to formal coaching arrangements.

We offer one closing point on this topic. Coaching is a *real* profession that requires *real* expertise. Successful coaching can make a difference in a leader's skills, development, and career, but not everyone will be a good coach. We all go to a doctor for medical advice or to an attorney for legal assistance. By the same token, coaching (internal or external) requires specific skills, and it should be appreciated for its professional contribution to leadership development. Excellent coaches build their expertise, toolboxes, and skills over years of experience. Although it may seem enticing to build an internal coaching program, companies should do so only if they are willing to build a talent pool as effective as external coaches.

Coaching Highlights	Organizations increasingly want to build internal coaching expertise given it has tremendous appeal in terms of reducing both costs and decreasing reliance on external resources. In this chapter, four organizations: The Progressive Group of Insurance Companies, Intel Corporation, Bell Canada, and Saudi Aramco provided insight into how their companies are building leaders and coaches internally.

- **The two main reasons to build an internal coaching pool** are (a) to replicate the high impact of external executive coaching at a lower cost, and (b) to provide better coaching for a specific assignment or a unique corporate culture.
- **Create a leader-as-coach program.** Organizations are increasingly interested in *leader-as-coach* programs to improve coaching skills, so bosses can assist leaders with on-the-job situations.
- **Mentoring.** Mentoring programs within a company can be effective to help leaders with certain challenges. They are not a substitute for coaching, however.
- **Weigh the pros and cons.** Companies thinking about creating an internal coaching pool should weigh the pros and cons, such as cost, experience, and credibility of coaches.

8 • Measuring Impact

Can you measure coaching's return on investment?

This is *the* question on the minds of coaching owners in all types of organizations. The return on investment (ROI) chase is this field's holy grail. Many have sought it, few have found it, and what they've found may not be it at all.

As coaching has evolved and companies have grown their programs, the expenditures have also grown. The increased expense has put a brighter spotlight on the value of coaching. Although some programs can get by with anecdotal evidence that coaching works, larger programs are subject to more intense scrutiny. In small companies, where the investment in coaching represents a more significant expenditure, the return on investment can be even more critical.

More and more we hear that organizational practitioners are being asked to quantify the value of coaching. The desire to learn more about impact metrics was a commonly cited reason why companies sponsored our original research in the first place.

Organizations have expressed a desire to measure impact, but they know it is also very difficult, or potentially impossible. One practitioner tells us that she doesn't bring up metrics—if she does, she might induce someone to question coaching's value.

But all holy grails aside, we found that many companies were quite behind in doing any form of metrics on their coaching efforts, let alone determining the return on investment.

Much corporate coaching lacks even basic metrics. A third of the organizations indicated that they *don't formally measure coaching impact*, and many organizational practitioners admitted that they could be doing more to measure impact. One noted that "[Measurement] is generally very much a subjective appraisal. I would like to see us move in the direction of going out and doing some more structured, though simple, measures, but we have not been doing that."

Here's an even more surprising finding: Leaders cared less about ROI—or any metrics for that matter—than organizational practitioners did!

If the leader was personally satisfied with the coaching engagement, that was often enough. If the leader was satisfied, the coach was generally satisfied. We found coaches somewhat interested in impact metrics, but not as concerned about it as organizational practitioners were.

Finally, we found that a vocal minority of companies don't respect ROI as holy grail. They recognize that coaching improves leadership capability, and they aren't concerned with attaching financial calculations to their efforts. They are not going to engage in the ROI chase.

Here is the key: Organizations are urged not to disregard coaching metrics. There are many useful options available. Although ROI is elusive, organizations need to employ the other proven techniques that are currently available. Otherwise, they lose a great opportunity.

In this chapter we offer a variety of ways to measure coaching results, including:

- Subjective measurements (satisfaction with coach, leader, and boss improvement evaluations);
- 360 follow-up feedback;
- Business result impact;
- Measurement tied to retention.

Start at Satisfaction with Coach

The first and most basic metric is to measure satisfaction with one's coach. This is a starting place that many companies have yet to implement. More than a third of our leaders told us that no one checked in with them regarding coach satisfaction. In one interview, we asked a leader, "Did your organization stay connected to your assignment?" The leader answered, "I have no idea."

Organizations report conducting coach satisfaction assessments more frequently. Approximately 65 percent of organizations told us that they gauge leader satisfaction with their coach by informally checking in with the leader. Another 27 percent of organizations conduct a quantitative satisfaction survey.

Obviously, this is an area for quick improvement. We suggest conducting a coach satisfaction evaluation a month into an assignment, and then quarterly thereafter. This provides the coach with early (and ongoing) feedback on the engagement. If there is a mismatch, the assignment can still be restarted relatively easily with a new coach.

Satisfaction surveys should be quick and to the point. One such online example is provided in Figure 18.

Figure 18.   Coach satisfaction survey.

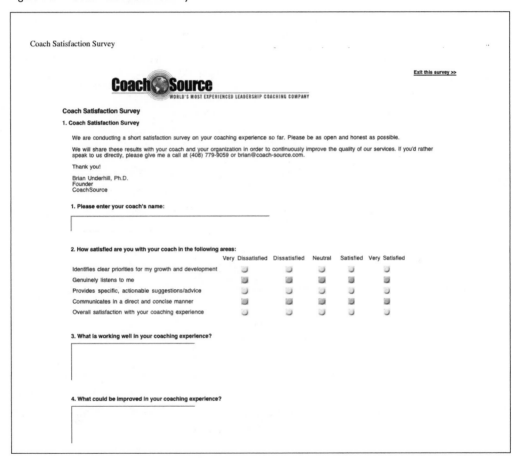

Include Impact Metrics

The most common impact metric is subjective: asking leaders if they thought the coaching was effective (Fig. 19). Organizations, leaders, and coaches all selected this option most frequently.

Figure 19.   Methods of measuring impact—organization, leader, and coach perspectives (select all that apply).

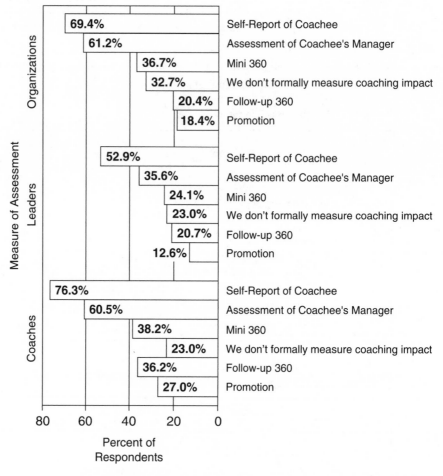

This is not a surprising result, because it is the simplest solution. If leaders feel they improved through coaching, it increases the possibility that other interested parties will be satisfied as well. Of course, this assessment is not tied to actual results, and it is completely subjective in nature.

Ask the Boss to Assess

The next option is to collect an assessment from the coachee's manager, and 61 percent of the organizations in our research did so. This method is the first step toward objective feedback, because the manager is more removed from the inter-action. He or she can judge whether or not improvement has been made. Often, if the manager is satisfied, it is likely that most of the other parties will be as well.

The boss assessment is still just one of many possible perspectives, however. After one recent coaching assignment, our leader improved as judged by his direct reports. But the manager, who was quite dissatisfied with his progress, did not agree. Our solution was to extend the coaching assignment until the manager noticed improvement.

This assessment by the manager approach is an improvement, but it is not fool-proof.

Follow-up with Another 360

Readministering a 360 feedback instrument is a more comprehensive option that is practiced by 20 percent of organizations. This approach requires conducting an original 360 prior to the assignment (the baseline), and another 360 either at an interim step or at the conclusion of the assignment. The feedback generally requires including the same respondents in both 360s.

The best option we've found is a mini-360 (currently selected by 37% of the organizations). A mini-360 (see Fig. 20) measures perception of leader improvement over time, focusing on only the specific areas for development chosen by the leader. With a mini's improvement scale, surveying the exact same rater group each time is not necessary. The survey is much less time-demanding on raters, and results can be aggregated among many leaders for a good view of overall improvement.

Measure Return-on-Investment

Return on investment (ROI) remains an elusive goal of the coaching industry. A desire for ROI is understandable. In fact, we applaud this objective and welcome any opportunity to showcase the benefits of coaching.

Given the fast growth of the coaching industry, it can be a challenge to justify the increasing expenditures if the benefits can't be quantified. One leader describes coaching outcomes in this way: "In most businesses we run by bottom-line performance measurement . . . it sure would be nice to have more crunchy, quantitative performance data."

A vast majority of organizations do not measure coaching ROI, but most (72%) would like to find a link (Fig. 21). As one organization reports, "This is our year of metric, so we are really interested in looking a little bit deeper at measuring it [ROI], and we haven't really addressed it yet."

However, 21 percent of organizations selected *no, and we don't believe a link is possible* when asked if they linked coaching and ROI. This strong minority of organizations felt that ROI was too difficult to measure, and they were not going to even attempt it. One organization representative said, "I am not surprised at all

Figure 20.   Mini-survey report.

Mini-Survey Report
Joe Sample

Rater Groups

Self 1   Direct Reports 5   Peers 4   Other Colleagues 0   Supervisor 1   Upper Management 0

In the past six months, has this leader asked for input from you concerning how he/she can improve?

	Yes	No
Direct Reports	5	
Peers	1	3
Supervisor	1	
	70%	30%

Over the past six months, how often has this leader followed-up with you concerning how he/she could improve?

	None	Little	Some	Frequently	Constantly
Direct Reports			2	3	
Peers	1	2	1		
Supervisor				1	
	10%	20%	30%	40%	0%

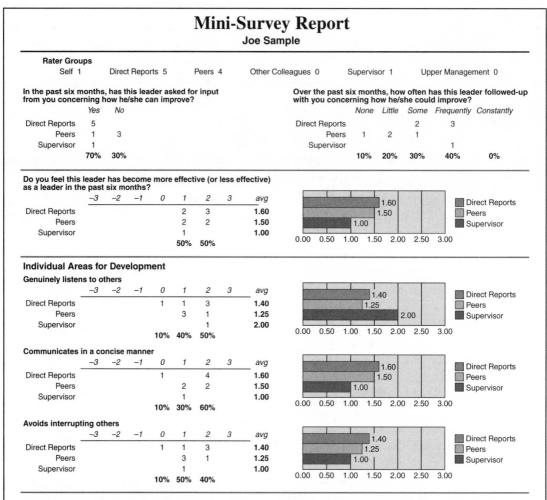

Do you feel this leader has become more effective (or less effective) as a leader in the past six months?

	−3	−2	−1	0	1	2	3	avg
Direct Reports						2	3	1.60
Peers						2	2	1.50
Supervisor					1			1.00
						50%	50%	

Individual Areas for Development

Genuinely listens to others

	−3	−2	−1	0	1	2	3	avg
Direct Reports				1	1	3		1.40
Peers					3	1		1.25
Supervisor						1		2.00
				10%	40%	50%		

Communicates in a concise manner

	−3	−2	−1	0	1	2	3	avg
Direct Reports				1		4		1.60
Peers					2	2		1.50
Supervisor					1			1.00
				10%	30%	60%		

Avoids interrupting others

	−3	−2	−1	0	1	2	3	avg
Direct Reports				1	1	3		1.40
Peers					3	1		1.25
Supervisor					1			1.00
				10%	50%	40%		

What has this leader done in the past several months that you have found particularly effective...

Direct Reports
- Gives precise next steps. Seems more prepared for 1-on-1's.
- Quicker turn around time. Less focus on minutia and more on larger picture. Better communication of expectations during 1x1s.
- He scheduled one on one meetings weekly for 1 half hour but after about 4 meetings realized that biweekly meetings for one hour better suited my needs. I am confident with his directions and feel that he attends to me and works toward helping me develop my skills.

Peers
- He will restate what he has heard from peers, thereby letting them know that they have been heard.
- His flexibility and ability to adapt to the current situation has proven to be highly effective.
- He has demonstrated the ability to flex his style to that of the person he is working with.

Supervisor
- He is very introspective, he thinks about a situation, processes what occurred and looks for ways to change behavior if appropriate.

What can this leader do to become more effective in the areas of development noted

Direct Reports
- Send emails or write suggestions. Not all of us have good auditory memory and it would be helpful to have specific suggestions in writing.
- I can't think of any specific examples or suggestions to become more effective. He is very visible and available to me daily. I feel as if Joe is always working toward knowing my work style and helping me to improve.

Peers
- Seeking input and assistance.
- He can continue to work on his flexibility and request feedback on what he needs to do differently to improve.

Supervisor
- Continue to work on organization and crisp communication.

Figure 21.   Linking coaching to level 4 (ROI) impact—organization perspective.

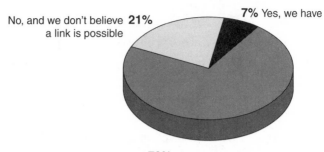

No, and we don't believe **21%**
a link is possible

7% Yes, we have

72% No, but we would like
to find a link

by the results that few companies are looking for ROI—I am in the 'forget it'
camp." A coach added, "[I] have not seen a decent ROI study."

There have been some strides made toward an ROI solution. As one organization told us, "We have linked developmental planning, as well as all of our
leadership development, to ROI with metrics—on different categories of profitability, growth, and use of assets—and we're getting some pretty interesting
data back."

In one method, leaders are interviewed (usually by an objective party) regarding the business metrics they feel coaching has impacted. Leaders are then asked
to determine the percent of impact attributable to coaching. A study by
MetrixGlobal[1] using this method found 584 percent ROI for a coaching program
at Nortel.

Manchester Consulting's[2] similar study found a six times benefit for leaders
coached. Leaders reported gains in productivity, quality, organizational strength,
customer service, reducing customer complaints, retaining executives who
received coaching, cost reductions, and bottom-line profitability.

A few organizations are calculating ROI based on improved retention of
coached leaders. The dollar value of each departed executive can be calculated, so
retaining more of these executives as a result of coaching would yield a positive
ROI figure. One company calculated a greater than 600 percent ROI, a figure influenced greatly by one executive who said he would have left if not for coaching.

Academics and statisticians are quick to point out that these ROI methodologies
are still subjective—the leader is offering his or her estimate of coaching's impact
on business metrics. Such an estimate does not absolutely measure actual business
impact. The truth is, there are many factors influencing key business metrics, which
makes it difficult to determine coaching's role. But to some organizations, this
approach is sufficient.

In employing a measurement approach, an independent party could carry out the ROI survey. Internal finance staff, internal industrial/organizational psychologists, or external consulting firms could all assist. This reduces any potential influence on the results by those attached to the outcomes.

Sony offers one example of how impact is measured. The corporation uses a technology platform to encourage leader follow-up, then asks leaders to estimate the percent value attributable to coaching.

Measuring the Impact

Deborah Swanson
Sony Corporation

As the saying goes, *what gets measured gets done*. At Sony, we believe in providing leaders with the tools to track their own developmental progress while also monitoring the progress of our programs.

One tool that has proved useful is *Friday 5s*. This is an online tool, created by Fort Hill, that allows leaders to identify and track the progress and results of their learning goals. Each participant completes a goal sheet at the end of our Leadership Forum and Leadership Curriculum programs. On the goal sheet each leader chooses two learning goals, creates an action plan, and identifies a metric for measuring business impact. Each goal involves work on a real initiative, targets a key competency (e.g., cross-functional collaboration or execution of strategy), and identifies one metric for measurement. The metrics for our Leadership Forum include: (1) growth-impact on new products or services; (2) profitability—impact on margins, SGA; (3) invested capital—impact on accounts receivable, inventory; and (4) leadership effectiveness. An example of a goal sheet follows (see Fig. 22).

All goal sheets are put into the Friday 5s system and tracked for a minimum of ten weeks. Every two weeks the leader receives a reminder to update his or her progress in the system. Sony's participation in all five progress updates surpassed other companies using Friday 5s, breaking records at 84%. The reasons can be primarily attributed to our follow-through, coaching, and design of wrap-up sessions with business head involvement.

Final questions in the system will ask participants to estimate the annual financial impact of their efforts and projects. To be even more accurate, we then ask them what percent of this financial impact is directly attributed to what they learned. In other words, what is the return on investment (ROI) for the program, the coaching received during the week, and the development over ten weeks. In 2005, leaders believed there was a $149 million positive impact on savings, growth, and improvements in effectiveness to the company—a strong link between leadership development and the bottom line.

Figure 22.   Leadership forum goal sheet.

 SEL Leadership Forum Goal Sheet

Please Print Clearly

Your Name: _____   Date: _____

Phone: _____   Team Name: _____-

Your Email Address: _____

Manager's Name: _____   Manager's Email: _____

Your manager will receive a copy of your goals. You will be able to send him/her your progress reports for feedback and advice.

(Optional)
Peer Coach's Name: _____   Peer Coach's Email: _____

If you designate a coach, you will be able to send him/her your progress reports for feedback and advice.

Write out your goals below. Check the category that best fits your goal. Your goals will be visible on the follow-through site to other members in your program.

Goal 1   **Objective:** {Describe the benefit or pay-off}.

In the next 10 weeks, my action plan will be to: {Describe your actions}	**Indicate ONE Goal Category:** ☐ Cross-functional collaboration ☐ Execution of strategy ☐ Great Place to Work Issues ☐ Business, Financial Acumen ☐ Navigating Change ☐ Other Leadership Behaviors
My measure of success/business metric I'm looking to impact is: {Describe what will be evident to others}	**Indicate ONE Business, Leadership Metric:** ☐ **Growth** — impact on new markets, products, services ☐ **Profitability** — impact on SGA, gross margins ☐ **Invested Capital** — impact on inventory, A/R, PPE ☐ **Leadership Performance** — any improvement that has increased effectiveness

Goal 2   **Objective:** {Describe the benefit or pay-off}.

In the next 10 weeks, my action plan will be to: {Describe your actions}	**Indicate ONE Goal Category:** ☐ Cross-functional collaboration ☐ Execution of strategy ☐ Great Place to Work Issues ☐ Business, Financial Acumen ☐ Navigating Change ☐ Other Leadership Behaviors
My measure of success/business metric I'm looking to impact is: {Describe what will be evident to others}	**Indicate ONE Business, Leadership Metric:** ☐ **Growth** — impact on new markets, products, services ☐ **Profitability** — impact on SGA, gross margins ☐ **Invested Capital** — impact on inventory, A/R, PPE ☐ **Leadership Performance** — any improvement that has increased effectiveness

Whereas Sony sought to measure actual return on investment, another research effort by Mary-Wayne Bush involved interviewing executives to see how they defined effectiveness.

What Makes Executive Coaching Effective?

Mary Wayne Bush
The Foundation of Coaching; Raytheon

Executive coaching is known to increase leaders' productivity and satisfaction, and results from a recent doctoral study by Mary Wayne Bush at Pepperdine University help us understand why. Bush interviewed 12 executives from multinational, for-profit organizations. Each of them had completed a coaching engagement that the executives described as effective. The study results identified six factors that made the coaching experience effective, from the coachees' point of view.

1. The coachee's commitment;
2. The coach's contribution;
3. Having a structured development process;
4. Including others in the process;
5. Having positive rapport and relationship with the coach;
6. Getting results that benefit the coachee.

Study participants agreed that in order for executive coaching to be effective, the coachee has to demonstrate readiness and willingness to be coached. A second key factor for effectiveness was the coach's contribution—characteristics such as the coach's frankness, positive attitude, and respect for the client's style and personality.

Also, the study respondents appreciated the fact that the coaching process was structured and focused on their development. Another factor in effectiveness was the inclusion of others besides the coach and coachee in the coaching process. Several of the executives reported developing their coaching goals based on feedback they got from others and sharing their goals with a select group of others who assessed their progress over time. They said that this process was helpful in gaining support and accountability for their progress, as well as encouraging and motivating them toward their goals.

The relationship and rapport between coach and client was shown to be central to coaching effectiveness, with executives reporting a strong bond of respect and caring in the coaching interaction.

The bottom line for all the study participants was that effective coaching produces results that benefit the coachee—both business and personal outcomes of coaching were identified as important. The message was clear that when the whole self is engaged through coaching, the outcomes are beneficial for the organizational system as well as for the individual.

The Bottom Line

For most organizations, there is still an opportunity to incorporate basic impact metrics. In terms of percentage of utilization, none of the current metrics scored above 70 percent from organizations.

Leaders aren't experiencing much in the area of measuring impact. They did not select any option with much frequency—only *self-report* was chosen more than 40 percent of the time.

Leaders are generally less worried about impact metrics than organizations are, however. This finding runs contrary to the view that business leaders always demand a return on investment for any significant investment. Leaders often view coaching as a personal benefit, and thus are less likely to require ROI metrics. However, organizational representatives (such as HR or LD professionals) are feeling challenged more often to justify the cost of coaching programs.

Although good ROI metrics are not proven, basic metrics are still underused. A combination of leader satisfaction assessment, leader and boss effectiveness assessment, and a follow-up mini-survey should all be standard procedures in coaching assignments.

Even though measuring leader satisfaction with the coach is important, at least one organizational representative urged us to "measure the leaders, not the coaches." Another organization asked, "But what is the cost of *not* doing coaching?"

And while the debate on measuring impact continues, we are reminded of an appropriate quote from Albert Einstein: "Not everything that can be counted counts, and not everything that counts can be counted."

Coaching Highlights

Organizations are missing excellent opportunities to measure the impact of coaching. Assessing the leader's satisfaction with his or her coach, the leader's and boss's assessment of improvement, and the use of follow-up surveys and mini-surveys are often overlooked. Although some return on investment methods exist, they are generally not well accepted by the marketplace.

- **Get smile sheets early.** Measure leader satisfaction with his or her coach early into the process (e.g., 1 month into a 12-month program). Do this informally or with a written survey.
- **Ask the leader and the boss.** Measure impact by assessing the opinion of the leader and his or her boss at the conclusion of the program.

- **Measure impact by many raters.** Implement a short mini-survey to measure the leader's specific areas for development in the eyes of those working with the leader.
- **ROI: Get it or forget it.** Decide whether a return on investment calculation is absolutely necessary, given the difficulties in measuring ROI. If not, conclude this debate once and for all.

9 • The Art of Finding Qualified Coaches

With nearly anyone capable of hanging out a shingle and declaring himself or herself in the coaching business, organizations are constantly struggling to find the most qualified coaches for their executives. Organizations report that locating coaches is generally not difficult (depending on where in the world one is)—there are plenty of them available. The real difficulty is locating and properly screening the most qualified coaches for their particular assignments.

In our experience as coaches, we find that companies who have established programs (over five years old) have set criteria and screening processes that work well for them. This is reinforced by the fact that very few coach-leader relationships fail or need a coach reassignment. However, we also find that companies just starting out in coaching struggle a great deal with determining where to begin in finding the right coaches. So our conclusion is that the start-up of a new program is challenging, but maintaining it is not.

Our research will show how organizations find coaches and how they screen these coaches. We uncovered which criteria organizations use to screen coaches. But on the question of whether these criteria match the preferences of the leaders they are serving, the answer is "not necessarily."

This chapter will also provide insight from three companies on these issues. Thrivent Financial for Lutherans explains their model of using a one-source provider for coaches. BP will describe their coaching vendor selection process. Finally,

Unilever will share the rigorous assessment process they use to screen coaches.

Qualifications

Successful coaches are as diverse as one could imagine, so it is difficult to describe the perfect background. The *most likely* background of a coach includes an advanced education degree in a *people field* such as industrial, organizational, or clinical psychology, human resources or leadership development. But there is not one particular advanced degree for coaching. Coaches we know have masters' or Ph.D.s in business, sociology, or other fields.

The vast majority of coaches have some prior business experience, often in a line or staff position. A business background is often a prerequisite from both a credibility and qualification standpoint. Many coaches often come into coaching from company human resources or leadership development positions. They may have done some ad hoc coaching or naturally have coaching skills. As the company discovered coaching, these people were in the right place to move into coaching roles.

At the initial screening, there are foundational sets of skills and traits that seem to matter to all companies, and to all leaders. After that, there are specific elements that matter to specific assignments, leaders, or companies. Some of these traits were mentioned in Chapter 7 in comparing internal to external coaches, but we'll expand the discussion here.

As the information below shows, there can be many characteristics to examine before hiring a coach.

Foundational Characteristics of a Coach

- Has strong interpersonal and communication skills
- Conveys credibility and trustworthiness
- Is able to be objective
- Has the ability to maintain confidentiality
- Is perceived as qualified—may or may not have advanced degrees, experience, or certification
- Has the ability to give direct, honest feedback
- Is intelligent and insightful
- Has confidence and maturity
- Has integrity
- Experience and reputation as a coach

Preferred Traits for Specific Assignments

• Personal chemistry with leader
• The right temperament
• Has understanding of and fits with organization's culture
• Has experience in specific organization, industry, or business environment
• Has specific certifications, training, or methodology
• Has mastered the use of specific instruments
• Has specialization in an area
• Has a positive track record
• Is in the right geographic location
• Has appropriate life experience

Locating Coaches

Organizations report finding coaches to be relatively easy for most western countries. The majority of organizations (80%) look for coaches from their existing vendors, trusting coaches provided by their current providers. Over half of the organizational respondents also reported obtaining recommendations from other organizations (*see* Fig. 23).

However, coaches answering the same question provided different answers from those provided by the companies. More often, coaches thought they were being found by contacting companies or their leaders directly and being located through the Web.

Figure 23.   How do organizations find coaches?—organization & coach perspectives (select all that apply).

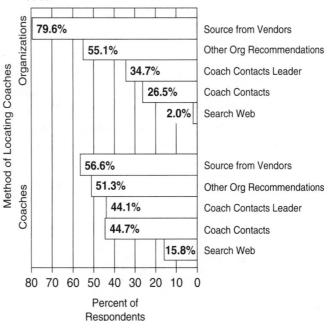

Certain geographic regions were identified as more difficult to locate coaches. Most notably, Japan, China, and India were regularly cited as difficult locations to find coaches. Organizations reported an expected increase in their use of coaches in China (especially Shanghai and Beijing), India (Bangalore), and Eastern Europe.

One option for finding coaches is to create an internal company process. The following is a description of BP's coaching vendor selection process.

Coaching Vendor Selection Process

Janet Weakland &
Bob Gregory
BP

At BP, a team from organizational & individual learning (O&IL) collaborated with procurement on a detailed coaching vendor selection process.

Our efforts started with a rigorous selection process asking potential suppliers to identify their service lines, to provide examples of past work and measures of its success, to identify their professional qualifications and certifications, and to describe their language and cross-cultural capabilities. This selection process resulted in an approved, diverse, and inclusive roster of more than 200 coaches with established contracts. We are now able to capture cost savings, driven both by competition among vendors and by the ability for BP managers to "comparison shop," and to make more cost-effective, informed choices.

In addition, we established a performance management process that allows us to track the effectiveness of the vendors and to make appropriate changes to the roster as time progresses. To give ease of access to our customers, the roster of approved coaching vendors is available through an internal Web site, which also provides information that potential users will find helpful when searching for a coach.

In the spirit of striving for operational excellence, we improved inefficiencies and enhanced existing processes. We took very inefficient procurement processes and established controls to secure, track, or manage coaching vendor management in a quantifiable manner to ensure wise spending on qualified vendors. In addition, we enhanced our capability to meet the increasing internal demand for resourcing external coaching vendors. Our efforts have resulted in the establishment of efficient processes that meet the needs of businesses and functions within the U.S. We estimate that an annual savings of fifteen to twenty percent, or $750K to $1.0M, will be realized by our efforts.

Another alternative is to use a one-source provider to find coaches. Thrivent Financial for Lutherans describes their partnership with such a provider.

Advantages for Using a Trusted Single Provider for Executive Coaching Sources

Kristin Olsen
Thrivent Financial for Lutherans

At Thrivent Financial for Lutherans we use a trusted single source to fulfill all our executive coaching needs for our sales leader organization. Here are the advantages for us:

- Face-to-face coaching arrangements for everyone in our geographically dispersed organization. By tapping into our provider's network, it became possible for us to quickly and easily provide face-to-face coaching anywhere in the U.S. that we had a need.

- Consistent experience for all of our leaders. All coaches adhere to the same coaching process and have access to the same set of assessment tools. Newly engaged coaches can also easily access past Thrivent Financial for Lutherans engaged coaches in their network to build their understanding about our organization and the role of our sales leader. We also jointly developed an *About Thrivent for Lutherans* description of our organization that is used during an initial conversation between the coaching firm and the coach in order to educate the coach about us and about our expectations for the relationship.

- Provided us quick acquisition of organizational knowledge and expertise about executive coaching. We had very little experience with executive coaching when we began our initiative, and taking advantage of our provider's expertise in this area built our capability and allowed us to get this initiative into place in a short time frame.

- Single contract and consistent pricing. Using a trusted single provider means just one contract and a single negotiated price for all coaching contracts. This streamlines our internal contracting process and makes it easier to predict our total cost for budgeting purposes. We also maintain just one primary relationship with the company, which allows for a *one-stop shopping* arrangement that helps us to efficiently maintain several coaching contracts at one time.

Screening Coaches

After locating coaches, there is still work to be done to screen and select the right coaches to work with the company.

Any company beginning a coaching process for the first time inevitably wonders, *what criteria should we use in screening coaches?* While many organizations have expressed worry regarding the difficulties in screening coaches, they had generally identified the suitable and relatively uniformly key criteria desired of their coaches.

How are coaches most commonly screened? Organizations generally begin the screening process by reviewing bios of potential coaches, some prescreened and referred by the vendor(s) working with them. Coaches are then interviewed in person or via telephone. "We have a set of behavioral criteria we use in coach assessment," says one organization. Another says they "Interview coaches and ask them to take us through a sample coaching session; then we debrief with them."

Figure 24.   Selection criteria for choosing coaches—organization, leader, and coach perspectives.

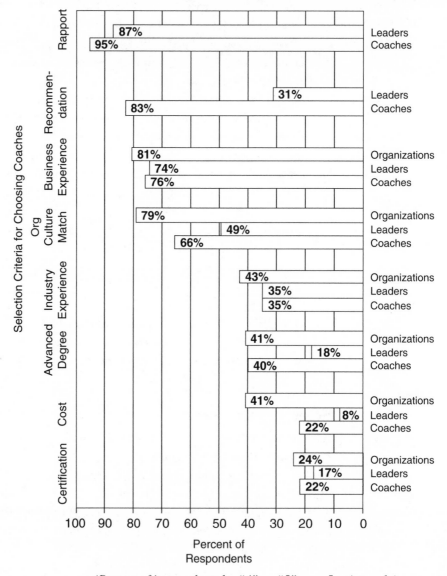

(Percent of items selected a "4" or "5" on a 5 point scale)

Organizations (Fig. 24) indicated *business experience* and *match with our culture* as critical factors in choosing a coach. Of lesser importance was *experience in our industry, advanced degree,* and *cost.* Specific certification was least important to organization survey raters. (Note: organizations were not asked about *ability to build rapport or recommendation from a colleague.*)

Leaders overwhelmingly selected *business experience* and *ability to establish rapport* as their top criterion in coach selection. *Advanced degree* and *certification* were minimally important, while *cost* came in last place. In interviews, leaders also identified "soft" traits in coaches, such as having a sincere desire and commitment to help, having adaptability and the right chemistry, being a good listener, becoming a trusted advisor, and having the ability to challenge back.

Coaches generally ranked all criteria as more important than did leaders, and coaches also strongly emphasized *ability to build rapport* and *recommendation from a colleague.*

In the following, Unilever will share the rigorous assessment process they use to screen coaches.

Unilever's Executive Coach Assessment Process

Sam Humphrey
Unilever

Unilever employs 230,000 people across 151 countries. In 2004, we developed and introduced a rigorous process for assessing executive coaches for Unilever.

The end vision was to create a diverse (in every sense of the word) pool of coaches that could be globally drawn upon, thus ensuring that both HR business partners and end users would have access to credible, competent coaches.

The start point was to get clarity on what we wanted to assess. We found that many coaches were very good at describing the work they did, but we did not know whether or not the coach was any good at coaching.

In developing the screening process, we engaged a consultancy specializing in developing professional coaches. I-coach also mirrored the values, ethics, and integrity that were important to us. We worked with I-coach to develop a set of coaching competencies and behavioral indicators that would be expected from coaches working at this senior level. These criteria then formed the basis of the assessment.

Our three stage process was:

Stage 1: Initial screening of biographical and technical data

Stage 2: Criteria-based interview (based on the five top-weighted criteria) (Unsuccessful coaches are offered some feedback after Stage 2)

Stage 3: A full-day assessment comprising presentation of the coaching framework, a coaching demonstration, and a final one-to-one meeting

Following Stage 3, all successful coaches receive an hour-long feedback meeting; unsuccessful coaches are also offered the opportunity for a feedback meeting. Over ninety percent of those who went through the process requested a feedback meeting.

Unilever chose to involve the end users in the process. Senior executives from around the business were invited to be trained as assessors and to take part in the process. Not only did their involvement in the process ensure that good coaches were selected, but it also increased executive awareness of what Unilever meant by good coaching.

The assessment process has been run six times in Europe and twice in Australia. To date, 69 coaches have been through the process, and 28 were invited to be part of the coaching pool.

Does Certification Matter?

There is a continually active debate in the coaching industry regarding certification. Of course, leadership development professionals in companies want to have the best coaches, but how do they determine who the best coaches are?

While certification could be the answer, today there is not a clear acceptance or standard for what this means.

The issue regarding certification seems actually to be more about coach qualification and standardization of practice, than about actual certification. One organization expressed it by saying, "I don't think that certification really correlates particularly well with effectiveness of coaching."

Our research clearly found that certification was of little concern for organizations and coaches, and that it was of virtually no concern for leaders. Just six percent of organizations *only use certified coaches*; and only 29 percent would *be more likely to use a certified coach*. Most leaders (63%) did not know whether their coaches held certification, nor were coaches certified (62% were not). One leader replied, "Sounds like a bunch of bull#$%@ to me."

Fewer than a third of organizations or coaches predict mandatory certification of coaches in the future. One organization stated, "I don't think we have any kind of certifying organization in the western hemisphere that is . . . worth anything." Another leader, when asked about certification, promptly said, "There is not widespread acceptance of any one certifying body as standard for the practice."

When asked which certification programs had the most credibility in the marketplace, only a few were noted. These included the International Coach Federation, Coaches Training Institute, Hudson Institute, and Newfield Network.

There is no doubt that certification leadership is still lacking. However, our experience is that there is some valuable learning inherent in nearly every certification program. We encourage coaches to continually develop and learn, whether through networks, conferences, or certifications.

Coaches should not expect a marked increase in their utilization or fees as a result of that certification, given that it is not viewed as necessary by organizations. But if corporations demand more certified coaches, the coaching market will respond. Clarifies one organization, "reliance on a standard certification credentialing is probably going to get more and more important, and I am not sure who's going to step forward and have the ultimate credentialing for this because this is such a fractionated industry." Another organization mentioned, "If there were a reputable certifying organization, we would love to have certified coaches! Certification does have more impact in the UK."

As you select coaches, we suggest reviewing their business experience, coaching experience, education, and instrument toolbox (*see* Chapter 5). Gauge their ability to build rapport as well. There are many temporary coaches who are in-between jobs or trying coaching as a possible career. These noncareer coaches will probably not have spent their time getting the right degree or instrument certifications, or building their toolboxes.

With all the focus on coach quality, one key successful coaching engagement ingredient sometimes overlooked is the leader being coached. One leader reminds us of the real point of this work: "Not all coaches must be great coaches. I've learned much from good coaches and from bad coaches. In sports, you don't have to have a good coach to learn. It is more about how you deal with the coaching that is the true journey. This process is about you and not about the actual process or methodology, or coach, for that matter."

Coaching Highlights	Companies beginning new coaching programs often struggle with determining how to find the right coaches. But companies with established programs of five or more years have criteria and screening processes that work well for them. So, while the start-up of a new program is challenging, maintaining it is not.

- **Rely on those you know.** Most organizations look for coaches from their existing vendors or obtain recommendations from other organizations.
- **Select your priorities.** The most critical factors in choosing a coach (for organizations) are *business experience, match with culture, experience in our industry, advanced degree,* and *cost.* Using a screening tool can enable

greater consistency and ensure that the right questions are asked when choosing a coach.

- **Certification.** Certification is not viewed by most organizations as an important factor for choosing a coach. Instead, focus on coach qualification and standardization of practice, rather than on actual certification.

10 • Creating a World Class Coaching Community

It's about community.

Build a community among your coaches; internal and external alike. With a modest investment in time and money, your coaching pool can share best practices, further develop their skills, and get closer to the company culture. These coaches will be more effective working for your company. And they tend to prefer working for those companies that make them a part of the community.

Why is this so important?

Coaches desire community. Coaches seek community. The nature of their work requires them to operate mostly one-to-one with a client, and not with many other people. Most are independent professionals—or affiliated with boutique firms—often working from home offices. In prior careers many worked in industry, so the transition to solo practitioner can be lonely. Coaches enjoy coming together on the phone, at a company site, or at the local coffee house to connect with other professionals.

Informal coach communities operate worldwide, inside and outside organizations. We've met members of such networks everywhere—telephone coaches in France, Coaches en Español (Latin America), Christian Coaches Network, Austin Coach Network, Intel's informal internal coach network, Alexcel Group, and Black Coaches Alliance. Some networks are for mutual learning and information sharing, but others are semiorganized businesses.

In our experience, coaches readily join an early Saturday morning learning conference call, eagerly share leads and tools with their peers, and often fly—at their own expense—to network gatherings. (It is not at all unusual for coaches to fly overseas for the same purpose.) All for the sake of learning and community.

Building a coaching community is a highly leveragable activity. But not enough organizations do it.

Why It Matters

On one hand, organizations should not be asked to create a community. The argument would be that because coaches are hired as independent experts, they are outside the company's responsibility. That's true. But the argument for creating a coaching community is that it actually benefits the company.

Coaches who feel connected to the company, and not just to the leaders they coach, have an enhanced sense of the company and its culture. When well-informed about company changes, coaches can incorporate these learnings into coaching assignments.

Stay Connected to the Pool

We asked organizations how they connected with their coaches. We examined various options, including informal conversations with coaches, regular conference calls, regular gatherings, and others.

None of the choices we offered scored above 54 percent (*see* Fig. 25).

We don't interpret this as a negative intent on the part of organizations. Further developing the coaching pool is usually an afterthought in the plan or comes later in building a coaching program. After a number of coaches work together, someone usually suggests, "Maybe we should have a conference call to share ideas and hear the latest news from the company." The first call is made, and all rate the experience valuable enough to do it more often. Other connection options then grow from there.

Nonetheless, the planful organization should think through connection options early in the process.

Community Conference Calls

Community conference calls are a simple, yet highly effective method for building community. Generally, calls are hosted monthly or quarterly, depending on the level of coaching activity. All coaches working with a given company are invited, or they may be subdivided by business unit, geographic region, or other criteria.

Figure 25. Keeping in touch with your coaching pool—organization perspective (select all that apply).

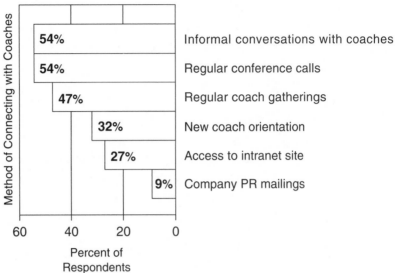

Generally, human resources, coaching manager(s), and/or the coaching vendor leads the call. Call content often includes:

• Quarterly financial update from the company
• Latest news, management, or structural changes
• Updates on coaching policies and activities
• Themes frequently encountered by coaches
• Case study review (learning from a specific coaching case)
• Best-practice sharing
• Coach discussion on company culture

Rules on confidentiality may need to be established for calls if sensitive matters will be discussed.

Using a Web-based slide viewer enhances the call experience. Recording the call allows access for coaches unable to attend (recordings can even be pushed out to coaches through a podcast).

Logistically, be cognizant of time differences. Rotate the start time to accommodate different geographies. Although telephone fees have fallen greatly, it is respectful to provide coaches (most especially those overseas) with a toll-free international dialing option.

Coach Gatherings

There is something magical about bringing coaches together for a gathering at the company site.

Coaches greatly enjoy the opportunity to learn more about the client and to share ideas with each other. Unprecedented community can be built. Coach loyalty to the corporation is greatly boosted.

Similar topics to those on the conference calls can be covered. Other ideas include:

- Presentation by executives regarding company strategy and objectives
- A leader to share firsthand his or her best-practice coaching experience
- Tour of company manufacturing or other facilities
- Certification in a specific instrument for use in the company
- Networking among coaches, company HR, and development personnel
- Special tourist outing unique to the host city

An underappreciated benefit for the in-person gathering is that company coaching owners get to know individual coaches more intimately. This greatly enhances matching of future assignments: company human resources and leadership development staff can make more accurate coach recommendations to coaching clients because they better know all parties personally.

As a practical matter, determine policies for reimbursing coach travel and time. Some companies pay for all travel and coach time; others share some costs with the coaches. Large multinational companies should consider regional forums as well.

Dell offers a great example of a three-day forum, featuring some of the above ideas.

Dell's First Annual Global Coaching Forum: Keeping the Partnership Strong

Kimberly Arnold &
Barbara Kenny
Dell, Inc.
Stephen E. Sass
Alliance for Strategic Leadership,
Coaching and Consulting

With our global coaching network firmly established and growing quickly, we recognized that the timing was right to bring together our external coaches and leadership development professionals from across the organization. The first Global Coaching Forum was held in April 2006.

Our intention was to bring all parties involved in coaching at Dell together to identify ways to continue to increase the effectiveness of coaching. Specific goals for the event were to:

- Strengthen the partnership between Dell and its coaching network.
- Increase our executive coaches' knowledge about Dell.
- Build community and encourage best practice sharing among coaches in the network.

- Familiarize coaches with assessment tools being introduced in our global leadership development programs.

The response to the invitation to attend was overwhelming. Despite the cost, coaches came from around the world: 27 came from the U.S. and Canada, four from Europe, and six from Asia/Pacific. Coaches were joined by approximately 25 learning and development professionals who played the role of "coaching owner" within their respective business units.

We structured the event to include a mix of networking, business, and best practice sharing.

- Day one included a review of Dell's business results with a senior finance executive, an overview of Dell's new global talent management/leadership development initiatives, and presentations from Marshall Goldsmith and Kate Ludeman, well-known executive coaches.
- Day two focused on best practice sharing, gathering feedback, and exploring emerging coaching needs at Dell.
- On day three, we offered certification on an instrument that Dell uses frequently in our executive leadership programs. The intention was to help coaches be familiar with this tool, because many of their leaders would have this additional source of data. External coaches who attended valued the opportunity to complete the certification as an added benefit of their relationship with Dell.

The forum was an incredible success. Dell was able to identify opportunities to enhance the current practice, gain an external perspective on development needs of our leaders, and gain better insight into the collective skills/abilities of our external coach partners.

As Dell shows, there are many benefits in the forum concept. Organizations of all sizes can reap the positive outcomes of the face-to-face forum.

New Coach Orientation

In some organizations, a robust new coach orientation program is created to better bring coaches into the fold. This can be a combination of face-to-face, telephone, and written materials. Content and materials to consider include:

- Documentation on coaching program
- Presentation by veteran coach(es) working at the firm

- Coaching templates (i.e., sample action plan form, interview protocol, feedback report example)
- Slides/notes from previous coach conference calls
- Company annual report
- Organization chart
- Corporate travel policies
- News and press releases about the organization
- Books written about the company (i.e., a book written by the company founder or CEO)

Coach-Support Web Site

Posting all materials on a coach-support Web site or company intranet eases administration. Coaches can gain 24/7 access to all the materials they need.

Company news, press releases, and notes/audio recordings of previous coach conference calls can be posted here as well.

Other Ideas

Adding coaches to physical or electronic corporate mailing lists enhances their ongoing knowledge of the company. Provide coaches with vendor ID badges for easier access to company facilities.

If you require coaches to travel, work to minimize the inconvenience and expense. Many clients provide access to the corporate travel department to ease the booking process and reduce expense. A best case option is to cover airfare and other expenses ahead of time, reducing coach out-of-pocket liabilities.

Johnson & Johnson, with over 230 operating companies, has found many ways to keep coaches better connected with the company.

Building Community with Coaches

Janet Matts
Johnson & Johnson

At Johnson & Johnson, we have several specific initiatives underway employing coaches. We now build special pools tailored to these efforts, using our current coach database, as well as any appropriately added talent.

Our Executive Leadership Survey (ELS) process for presidents and general managers in the medical device and diagnostics businesses, for example, has a hand-picked team of coaches that have extensive business coaching experience, dedication, loyalty, and great flexibility to support this fairly new initiative. Each business involved has a specific coach dedicated to it. This provides someone who is continuously building institutional knowledge and cultural awareness, as well as an invaluable familiarity with the leaders and their leadership teams, and with their HR business partners.

After a selection process, these coaches were part of a program-specific on-boarding program. We connect via monthly conference calls, and we have a core team available to support their integration, as well as business-specific program directors, and an HR resource assigned to coordinate and act as liaison. The network built as a result of the work by both the program director and the coach is dynamic and cumulative in both its knowledge and value.

With the recent rollout of our Global Leadership Profile (GLP), the associated 360° process is supported by an external feedback facilitator (for senior leaders). A CD that reviews the 360° and report, support for the process and positioning, is available to the operating company HR partners as they roll out the process. In addition, the external coach/consultant can provide support, shadowing, and practice for our HR partners, who provide internal feedback facilitator support (director and manager).

The executive coaching pool is always evolving. Often an operating company person has a recommendation or referral that we can add to the mix. Our coaching partners also provide a consistent, focused, and well-honed process in working with our operating companies.

We strive to build a community among the coaches. Although we don't get them *all* together, we do hold regional or operating company-specific gatherings with our teams of coaches. We host regular teleconference events. I personally spend a day per month meeting and connecting with coaches, and I also work with our regional people, assisting them in creating this same environment among their coaches in other regions of the world.

Develop Coaching Talent

In a recent conversation we had with a leadership development director, he said that he was troubled by the rapidly increasing number of executives he required in China within the next few years.

His challenge? There are very few qualified coaches in China. He had been in touch with nearly every major and boutique provider to no avail. There just simply aren't enough coaches to serve his future needs in China.

He suddenly said to us, "why don't we develop coaches in China just like we develop leaders?" In other words, *treat coach development similarly to leader development* in regions where talent is sparse.

The concept is to identify coaching talent in China and grow that talent to the same capability available elsewhere. Give candidate coaches increasingly higher-level assignments (with plenty of feedback), use a mentor coach to oversee their work, assist them in furthering their coaching training, offer additional instrument certifications, etc. All of this can be provided at relatively minor expense (especially compared to the expense of flying in a coach repeatedly from another region).

Too often, organizations require coaches to exceed each of their criteria, in all regions of the world. In some places, this just is not possible. Giving promising coaches a chance to develop through this option is a great idea.

In our experience, coaches would likely welcome this effort and would readily be a part of it.

Know How Coaches Tick

Coaches operate under a complex formula in determining whether to work for one organization or another. Many organizations falsely overrate the importance of the fees offered. We suggest otherwise.

Executive coaches are incredibly dedicated to their craft, and, as such, they are looking for meaningful work, the opportunity to grow, and a sense of connection.

Fees are not generally a primary driver for coaches. That does not mean that fees aren't important. They are. But many coaches will not hesitate to offer their services at a reduced rate or pro bono to a worthy friend or charity. We've seen world-class (and expensive) coaches work for a relative bargain for local assignments. Some coaches readily fire a well-paying client if the client misses too many meetings, or the client's companies take too long to pay.

Here are the types of questions coaches often consider in debating the merits of a particular assignment:

- Leader—What level of leader is this? What is this leader's functional area? Is this leader a high performer or a performance problem?
- Chemistry—How well do I connect with the leader? Is this leader a willing participant? Is this leader responsive to me?
- Organization—Is this a company I want to work with? Do they add value to my bio/CV? Would I prefer to work for a smaller company (benefit: make a potentially greater difference), a larger organization (benefit: bigger name for my biography), a government agency (benefit: serve the public sector), or a nonprofit (benefit: give back to the community)?
- Industry—Do I want to work in this industry? Do I want more experience in this industry? Do I have moral/ethical restrictions on working in this industry?
- Workload—How busy am I right now? Do I need to pick up more business, or do I have too much?

- Prior Obligation—How obligated do I feel to assist this client/company? Should I honor new requests because I have in the past? How has this client treated me in the past?
- Coaching Firm (if applicable)—Do I like working with this coaching firm? Do I want to do more work through this particular firm?
- Location—Do I have to travel to do this work? Would I like to travel to the location(s) requested? How easy is it for me to get to these locations from where I am? What are the company travel policies?
- Community—Is there a coach community at this company? Can I be a part of it? What type of challenge will this assignment provide?
- Fees—What are the fees? How long does it take to get paid? How difficult is it to get paid?

Organizations are smart to weigh all the different variables in calculating their overall offer to potential coaches. In this way, they can secure the most desirable and appropriate coaches for their needs.

Coaching Highlights

There are incredible benefits to building a strong community among coaches (internal and external). Enhanced learning opportunities, greater consistency among coach practices, and increased goodwill toward the organization are some positive outcomes. Additionally the organization gains an objective view of itself. Dell and Johnson & Johnson shared their experiences in building a coaching community.

- **Start smart.** Orient new coaches to the program, through face-to-face, telephone, and written materials.
- **Reach out.** Host coach community conference calls monthly or quarterly; cover the latest company financials/news, coaching policies, and common coaching themes; and share best practices.
- **Bring them in.** Bring coaches together for a forum; offer presentations by senior leaders, discuss common coaching themes, tour company facilities, and share best practices.
- **Simplify life.** Smooth out details for coaches. Add coaches to company mailing lists, provide them with vendor ID badges, and offer access to your company travel department.

11 • Life After Coaching

Is coaching really over when the contract expires?

The idea of coaching is often presented in the context of the time spent between leader and coach during the specific engagement. But coaching really continues on after the official assignment ends.

If successful, the coaching benefits will continue in the months and years after the engagement has ended. Insights and new behaviors live on well after the assignment is over. Leaders can do some amount of *self-coaching*, using the information and process learned during the coaching experience.

Along with this, we find coaches who maintain relationships with their leaders for quite some time after coaching. Often these relationships are informal coaching conversations for which the coach is not normally compensated. Coaches generally do this in an effort to be helpful to their former clients, although some may also hope to generate additional contracted work.

In all coaching engagements we always offer to be available following the assignment. Over the years, we've made this offer to several thousand telephone feedback coachees. In all honesty, only a small number of leaders actually take us up on the offer, and very few have abused it.

Nevertheless, the offer is on the table, and those with longer coaching experiences are more likely to take us up on it. We suggest that companies inform their leaders about the expectations and possibilities beyond the coaching engagement.

Based on his years of experience in managing coaching engagements, Harris Ginsberg further elaborates on the end of coaching interventions.

When Coaching Interventions Terminate

Harris Ginsberg
Chemtura Corporation

What happens when the coaching relationship comes to an end? The answer depends on whether the closure was mutual, if the objectives were met, and whether the protégé truly leveraged the opportunity to reflect, acquire, and master the skills or capabilities for which coaching was established in the first place. In any case, termination is as critical to success as the introductory meeting.

One senior executive was so invested in her learning through coaching that she actively adapted to three different coaches offered by the corporation over a six-year period of time as she continued to build her leadership capability and address some behaviors that periodically derailed her. Each coach established their own relationship. As internal coaches, they shared a common approach that allowed for continuity of coaching. The coaching ended only when the organization redeployed and withdrew the support.

The executive, who was deeply introspective and analytical, continues to recycle and harvest her learnings from the coaching relationships, essentially engaging in self-coaching. She has grown her business ten times larger than when it began and is developing her successors to continue the progress through a coaching style that supplements her strong drive for business growth.

Coaching ends in other ways as well, where less successful results have been achieved. When told that his coach was no longer available, one executive lamented, "Who will keep me on track?" His comment suggests that the coaching had not yet resulted in sustainable change. Other executives shrug their shoulders—possibly because they were less invested in the outcomes at the beginning. Others seek out their HR departments and ask for a new resource. At one company that eliminated leadership coaching in a reversal of its executive development strategy, executives have pursued coaching relationships under the radar screen.

Inevitably, leadership coaching is bound by time and commitment. Whether the coaching relationship terminates as a matter of course or as a wholesale shift in the corporate talent strategy, it is essential for coaches and protégés to discuss closure and to celebrate progress made during the intervention.

Renegotiate the Relationship

After a coaching engagement is officially over, it is essential that the relationship be renegotiated. The leader needs to redirect all of his or her efforts to the business, learning to incorporate coaching's objectives in everyday work. The coach needs to direct his or her time to other leaders and coaching engagements.

However, the relationship does not necessarily need to end forever. Most, if not all, coaches would welcome an opportunity to touch base to see how the leader is doing. Coaches we know take pride in their work with leaders. Hearing that the coaching has been successful through a follow-up conversation would be welcomed.

Coaches state that their engagements are lasting longer than what organizations report (*see* Chapter 4). One possible reason for the discrepancy is that organizations are referring to the actual contract time, whereas coaches reference the *relationship* time, which includes follow-up conversations after the contract ends.

Our experience also shows that leaders would welcome speaking to their coaches without worrying about the financial implications (if any). Leaders often assume that the coach is being compensated somehow through the company and that they are entitled to this continued interaction.

We propose a renegotiated relationship in which the coach is termed a *senior advisor* (an idea from Richard Leider).[1] The coach can be available for light, informal connections after the engagement's conclusion. Compensation for this senior advisor role can be built into the original contract.

A typical arrangement might call for the coach to be available for a certain number of telephone hours for up to a year following the end of the assignment. The leader can use the coach as a sounding board for ideas. Administration is simplified if these fees are in the original contract, or the coach service can be offered as an add-on option.

Boost the Fading Finish

Some coaching engagements limp across the finish line. Generally, the startup excitement has waned, the leader has incorporated some of the learnings, and coaching is mostly in maintenance mode. Meanwhile, normal business challenges take a greater priority. Scheduled calls and visits become less frequent as the leader's energy level declines (and sometimes the coach's, too).

We suggest ensuring that final metrics, such as a follow-up mini-survey, are part of the plan. This keeps all parties focused on the *final exam* of the process. Leaders are reminded of the imminent survey, and they'll want to finish strong.

This is also the time when leadership development and human resources, as well as the leader's boss, should reconnect with the concluding assignment. We find that many of them feel that the box has been checked, and they're on to other things—but a renewed connection is definitely in order at this point.

Coaches should watch for this fade, plan to boost their efforts, and request a final meeting that includes the leader, boss, etc. Knowing this is going to happen can usually boost the focus, and simply paying attention will usually sharpen the finish.

Internals Can Continue Support

If internal staff has additional bandwidth to contribute to the coaching work, we strongly support it. Building in a weekly quick connection can greatly enhance the leader's accountability toward achieving his or her stated goals.

Kevin Wilde, CLO at General Mills, describes how he continues a coaching engagement when the external coach has completed the *official* assignment.

Keep Coaching Alive From the Inside

Kevin Wilde
General Mills

As assignments with the external coach conclude, there is an incredible opportunity for the internal resource (the *internal*) to maintain progress. The internal, already included in the original contracting and in touch with the entire process, can then design and execute a follow-up regimen to reinforce behavioral change.

Most typically, the internal can meet or telephone the executive at regular intervals and inquire about continuous improvement in key behavioral areas. For example, I provided follow-up support for an executive after he had successfully completed a development engagement with an external coach. In one example, I met with the leader for about 15 minutes every Friday for three months. In each meeting, I asked him several specific questions, all based on his areas for development. The conversation then turned to any number of topics in support of these areas for development. This executive leader needed the reminding, and it would have been impractical (and costly) to ask the external coach to play this role. Moreover, the executive appreciated the support to help integrate what he had learned into his weekly routine, while being respectful of his time.

As administrators of coaching, internal resources often selflessly overlook the fact that they could be key recipients of the coaching experience *themselves*! Very few internals recognize or realize that they should also undergo development as a result of the coaching process. By doing so, the internals can add incredible value to the corporate process through their own experiences in coaching. This personal development outfits the internal resource with the experience and empathy needed to better guide coachees under his or her jurisdiction.

Wilde is onto a great idea. What an excellent opportunity for internal staff to keep the development moving once the external coaching has concluded.

Beware of Dependencies

A colleague tells us of one leader–coach assignment that has renewed itself every year for five years in a row. We hear that the leadership development people tried in vain to conclude the coaching after the second year, but without success.

This leader claims incredible value from the relationship and insists on continuing the coaching. However, as a VP/GM of the company's most profitable business line, this leader owns the budget for coaching. So if he wants to continue, that's what will likely happen.

This brings up an important point—dependency.

Dependency happens when the leader uses a coach indefinitely without active plans to conclude the assignment. Signs that dependency may be occurring are:

- Prolonged engagements lasting more than 2 years, unless the areas of development change;
- Slow progress on developmental goals;
- Frequently referring to the need to "discuss this with my coach," or reliance on the coach's advice by waiting to make a decision.

If you suspect that dependency is occurring, our advice is to talk openly about it with both the leader and the coach. Ask about the specific goals and success metrics, or confirm when the coaching assignment is expected to end.

Responsible coaches understand that leaders must be prepared to continue on their own, and they will work themselves out of the assignment.

Self-Coaching

Coached leaders ought to know that their development is an ongoing process—a never-ending one, at that. Plans for their ongoing development after coaching should be clear to them.

Good coaches will conclude an assignment by pointing the leader toward new or refreshed development objectives. These goals are inspired by final survey results, boss input, or the leader's own discretion.

In one six-month engagement, the leader accomplished fairly good improvement scores on the follow-up survey. However, his area for development—being a better delegator—was such a new behavior for him that he felt compelled to keep building on what had already been started. The coach refreshed his action plan with him by adding new steps, enhancing higher-impact actions, and removing less-useful items. To this day, the leader continues working the steps in the plan, even without the coach.

The best coaching processes encourage leaders to dialogue openly—and on an ongoing basis—with key stakeholders regarding their development objectives (*see* Chapter 4). This keeps the feedback and change process underway. Leaders can continue this dialogue with raters even after coaching has completed. They can have quick quarterly conversations with key stakeholders to inquire whether or not they have continued improving in their areas for development.

Keep Measuring

Even when formal coaching is complete, leadership metrics should continue.

Impact metrics originally conducted during the assignment can be refreshed after coaching is complete. In fact, a mini-survey instrument can be run easily every six months. We don't want to over-survey the raters, so we suggest a full 360 repeated no less than every 24 months, with much shorter mini-surveys in between.

A simple schedule such as this keeps leader development a priority, even when coaching is not active.

Coaching can and should continue after the official engagement is complete. It is most successful when an internal coach can continue the support, when leaders pursue self-coaching, and when metrics continue to measure the results.

Coaching Highlights

The benefits of successful coaching can continue after the official engagement has ended. Leaders can practice *self-coaching*, using the information and process learned during the coaching experience.

- **Inform leaders about the opportunities.** Companies should inform their leaders about the expectations and possibilities beyond the coaching engagement. More often than not, coaches make themselves available for follow-up conversations with leaders.
- **Support from Leadership Development and Human Resources.** Both can provide support after the assignment ends by following up with the leader, ensuring accountability, and possibly even offering additional coaching.
- **Beware of dependency.** One caution is to be aware of leaders who become dependent on their coach without active plans to conclude the assignment. Responsible coaches should help prepare leaders to continue on their own.
- **Continue the coaching.** Coaching is most successful when an internal coach can continue the support, when leaders pursue self-coaching, and when metrics continue to measure the results.

12 • The Future of Coaching

Where is the industry going? Is coaching a fad that is here today, gone tomorrow? What will the practice of coaching look like in the future?

Executive coaching has really only just begun. The increasing demand for leadership development, growth of coaching assignments the past 10 years, and interest in internal coaching are all evidence of momentum in the field.

In this chapter we will forecast the future of the coaching industry. Based on our experience and on conversations with thought leaders, corporate practitioners, and coaches, as well as on our research findings, we've formulated a number of conclusions on the future of this industry.

Practice Standardization

We believe there will continue to be a movement toward creating standardization in certain aspects of coaching, but not to the level of replacing the expertise of the coaches in an assignment. We don't know of anyone who attempts to control the actual conversations between a leader and coach.

Organizations with longer-standing programs have already moved toward creating consistency in the terms of assignments. This includes length of coaching assignments, proprietary 360° instruments, screening coaches, and more standardized rates and contracts.

One organizational practitioner summed it up by saying, "There needs to be some commonly accepted standards of professional practice of executive coaches, just as there are accepted standards of professional practice of psychology, law. . . ."

Results Focused

What companies are really looking for is results. The discussion about certification, selecting the right coaches, and how to measure impact is all due to a focus on results. As one coach told us, "What executives look for is impact. They have lots of people offering them advice, . . . but having someone who actually can have an impact quickly, and it's a good use of their time, is hugely important to them."

With results-guarantee contracts, this takes away some of the concern, and we believe more companies will demand such an arrangement. Similarly, greater focus on some of the basic metrics discussed in Chapter 8 is likely to expand.

An exciting trend we anticipate is a more integrated approach of coaching with succession planning. Many companies have moved toward this, and by doing so, they are able to track whether their programs are successful by simply looking at their succession pipeline.

New Forms of Coaching

We see many new kinds of coaching emerging.

Leader-as-Coach

Increasingly organizations are interested in teaching their leaders to be better coaches on the job, a *leader-as-coach* concept. We see a rise in the number of training programs with this aim in mind. Organizations are seeking to engender a more robust coaching culture by equipping their leaders as coaches with coaching skills.

At the simplest level, leaders coach their direct reports either on performance management coaching, or on task-specific issues. A coach-savvy leader will likely do a better job in performance-managing direct reports.

Enhancing a leader's coaching skills as part of his or her overall development is an excellent step in the right direction. It allows for *just-in-time* coaching, on a daily basis, and with practical application for work issues.

However, a professional coach offers greater objectivity and confidentiality. So while leader coaches are a great enhancement, there will always be a need for the objective, formal coaching role.

Team Coaching

One of the newest evolutions in coaching is working with a team of people simultaneously. This is one way to economically bring coaching to an organization, while helping a team work together more successfully. Generally one coach works with multiple leaders of a team, usually conducting separate meetings, or working within a group meeting format.

This approach expands coaching to more participants. It also creates a very positive *we're all in this together* mentality, encouraging leaders to assist each other. We like this approach in situations in which there is a true team need. This approach can work for an executive team, work team, or functional group.

However, this format does lack full-confidentiality boundaries, as other members would be privy to conversations. Leaders may be less likely to reveal deeper details needed for a full, formal coaching process. Also, as Chapter 4 points out, pairing the same coach to multiple leaders may not create the best matches.

Peer Coaching

Peer coaching is a simple accountability concept proposed by Marshall Goldsmith. In it, leaders coach each other in pairs. Each duo connects by phone daily, for a maximum five-minute call. Leader one asks leader two a series of questions relating to leader two's development objectives. They then switch places and repeat the process.

Ahead of time, each participant defines which questions he or she would like to answer. For example, a leader looking to improve his listening skills might design his questions this way:

> *"How many times did you rephrase what someone said to you today?"*

> *"Did you interrupt anyone today?"*

> *"How did you do as a listener today, on a one-to-ten scale?"*

The key is that each question should require a yes/no or numerical answer. The inquiring leader simply records the answers provided each day and feeds back a summary at the end of the week. The simple fact that there is daily measurement—by another person—makes a large difference in motivating people to change.

Peer coaching can be taken much farther, covering not only business, but personal daily goals as well. Sample personal questions could include these questions:

> *"Did you exercise 20 or more minutes today?"*

> *"How many hours of sleep did you get last night?"*

> *"How many minutes did you spend with each child?"*

> *"Did you relax/meditate/pray today?"*

As long as daily measurement is being conducted, measuring multiple aspects of life is possible.

Developmental Coaching

How deep should coaching go? Leadership coaching generally includes clear objectives with specific skills to work on during an assignment. But there has been discussion the past few years relating to deeper levels of coaching.

By addressing deeper levels of coaching, we still mean sustainable change, but without a specific developmental area in mind.

Bill Hodgetts of Fidelity Investments shares his views on developmental coaching and encourages us all to think beyond leadership coaching.

Developmental Coaching

William Hodgetts, Ph.D.
Fidelity Investments

Developmental coaching aims at fostering a deeper transformation in the executive. Developmental coaching can significantly accelerate a leader's development by increasing his/her self-awareness and generating more complex ways of understanding his or her world.

Many leadership studies suggest that leadership effectiveness and self-awareness are closely linked. Research done at the Center for Creative Leadership (and elsewhere) has long confirmed a strong tie between executive derailment and lack of self-awareness. Developmental coaching, by strengthening this key area, is therefore likely to strengthen leadership capacity.

Developmental coaching:

• Deals with the executive as a *whole person*, looking at all aspects of his/her life
• Is *deeper*—executives gain awareness of deeper, and perhaps, previously hidden parts of themselves
• Moves towards greater personal honesty, authenticity, and integrity
• Views the coach/leader relationship as a catalyst for deeper developmental change
• Is transformational—what changes is an executive's core identity
• Is longer term, with coaching lasting one or more years

Initially, behavioral and developmental coaching may be similar. The behavioral coach would focus on specific client behaviors to strengthen or weaken. Once these behaviors had adjusted to acceptable levels, the work would be essentially completed.

The developmental coach might initially use a behavioral approach, however, this would be only the first step. As trust grows, the coach might begin probing the client's implicit basic assumptions about self and world, and examine the linkage between those assumptions and the problematic behaviors that may have initially led to the coaching engagement. Over time, the coach would provide a safe place for his client to reflect on, examine, and potentially change some of his or her deepest, most closely held assumptions and beliefs about operating in the world.

This kind of deeper work cannot be rushed, because its effectiveness depends on the client's readiness to examine his or her life at this more fundamental level. A good developmental coach never forces his or her insights on clients, but rather offers the space and opportunity to do this deeper work only when and if the client is ready to engage at this level.

What is needed is a new kind of contingency model of coaching which views this work on a continuum from behavioral to developmental. This gives us guidelines for determining which kind of coaching is appropriate in which kinds of situations. Organizations and executives need both kinds of coaching, but ignore the developmental kind at their own risk!

Regulation

Certification

As shown in the research, certification of coaches is not a significant factor in the corporate marketplace. The majority of participants do not expect certification to become mandatory in the future, but they would be open to the idea if an organization would do it well.

Richard Leider predicts that we will see a movement toward standards. He says, "we [will] either police ourselves as a profession, or we [will] get policed. It is only a matter of time."

Again, we propose designing an accepted standard for executive coaches, which will likely vary from International Coach Federation standards (which tend to be more life coaching focused). Rather, these standards would be more applicable to executive coaches working in organizations.

We expect there will be lively conversations around certification. While certification is still the subject of active debate, we believe that as executive coach qualifications become clearer, the discussion of certification will start to quiet down.

Coaching through Technology

Technology is moving forward at such great speeds it seems obvious it can and will be used more frequently in coaching. The following are examples of how we expect to see technology in coaching.

Online Follow-Up Tools

We see a trend toward using software to track leaders' development progress. One example—mentioned in Sony's piece on metrics (*see* Chapter 8)—Fort Hill's Development Engine[1] is a tool that enhances goal accountability through technology.

Leaders declare their goals and key action steps; then they send requests to their managers, coaches, and other key stakeholders for input. On a regular basis (every one to two months), the system asks leaders for updates to their progress. Coaches can interact with their leaders between coaching sessions, using the tool. Group progress can be tracked easily.

We've found such technology an excellent enhancement to ongoing coaching contracts where contact isn't as frequent as might normally be desired.

Simultaneous Document Viewing

Creating and editing documents can now be done simultaneously and instantaneously online (i.e., docs.google.com). In this way, the coach and leader can both virtually view and update the action plan, metrics, checklists and other documents in real time.

There can often be a difference between discussing a concept and putting that concept into words agreeable to both parties. In this manner, action steps, ideas, and other items can be jointly edited on the screen until crystal clear.

Video-Assisted Coaching

We are excited at the enhanced video-assisted capability in the marketplace today.

Years ago, we worked to conduct a coaching session via videoconferencing. The coach was in San Diego, the coachee in San Jose. We each left our offices and drove 20 minutes to different videoconferencing facilities, and waited while the ISDN system was being tested by the techs. Finally, we began our call. The picture was good, the echo annoying, and the bill several hundred dollars to both of us.

Decent videochat technology already exists on most computer desktops. It is possible that in the near future PCs will ship with built-in videocams. Telephone coaching can now be enhanced with video images. In fact, we plan to begin interviewing overseas coaches exclusively via videochat as soon as the technology is suitably distributed.

Industry Trends

Taming the Wild West

A few years ago, a Harvard Business Review article[2] described the coaching industry as being like the *Wild West*. Our experience and research tell us that many organizations actually have fairly well-defined processes, standards, and practices in place, and they are succeeding with their current programs. Granted, companies just beginning coaching programs will go through a learning cycle, but a lot of information and guides (such as this book), will make their learning curve much faster. Furthermore, the Wild West was eventually tamed, and that appears to be the pattern in the coaching industry.

The concern about coach quality isn't totally justified, and it will ease over time as less skilled (and thus less successful) practitioners exit the industry. Many other industries have seen the same trends early in their development (i.e., early railroads, automobile manufacturers, the dot com boom, etc.). Eventually the influx of less-talented providers is corrected as the industry matures.

Provider Trends

Coaching providers have settled into a mixture of large firms, virtual organizations, local boutiques, and independent coaches. This is very similar to the way the consulting businesses grew to what it is today. Our research showed that a majority of respondents do not expect the coaching industry to consolidate (as some have predicted).

One trend we are seeing is outplacement and executive recruiting firms buying or launching coaching businesses. These companies see coaching as a complimentary offering to their other services. As such, a coaching component is a means to expand their offerings to existing clients.

Geographic Trends

Organizations are increasingly seeking qualified coaches located near their worldwide facilities, rather than paying travel expenses. The industry has already developed in such a way that ample coaching talent is available in the most common markets.

However, there are still coach shortages in key markets, such as in China, India, and Japan. We expect this to correct itself as the natural dynamics of supply-and-demand take effect.

Coaches are also difficult to locate in Eastern Europe. A developed, independent, free-agent marketplace of coaches is generally necessary to sustain a coaching presence in countries. Again, this could correct itself if the market demands it.

Closing Thoughts

Our experience, research, and current trends fully indicate that executive coaching is not just a fad, but here to stay. In fact, it will grow.

Of the organizations we surveyed, only two percent plan to decrease their use of coaching over the next five years. That means that 98 percent expect to either use the same level of coaching or to increase it. Over 92 percent of leaders who've been coached indicate that they'll hire a coach again when the time is right.

The pressure on corporations to bolster their talent pools has never been greater. The aging population in the United States shows a shortage of talent as baby boomers begin to retire. Consequently, attracting, retaining, and developing talent will become an increasing challenge. Former Secretary of Labor, Robert Reich,[3] recently commented that the only real source of competitive advantage for any corporation is, (1) its brand, and (2) its people—and people are what define the brand. Nearly any other differentiator can be copied by competitors. Consequently, investing in people development will be critical.

Companies have an opportunity to enrich the lives of their leaders through coaching. One executive in our research summed it up by saying, "If you have coaching done well, you change your life, and your life as a business leader. If you have the right coach with the right fit, he or she can make a tremendous impact, and a good coach can get you there."

Leadership development will continue trending toward on-the-job development, rather than pulling executives away from their daily responsibilities. At a learning forum, former Agilent Technologies CEO Ned Barnholdt once mentioned that he did not have time to leave his posts during his career, and that he hadn't been to an offsite leadership development exercise in over 20 years. Learning will need to be more *on-the-fly*, and executive coaching will play a role in this effort.

The executive coaching industry has come of age. Like many other industries, there will continue to be further definition of the practice, standardization of procedures and a differentiation of providers. It will become clearer what *hiring a coach* represents.

But perhaps the most likely trend is that coaching will continue to serve as an on-the-job replacement for more traditional methodologies. Internal and external training, both listed as the most likely substitutes for coaching, will experience a shift as more content is delivered through coaching. The increased use of internal coaches will continue to deliver and reinforce this content as well.

Executive coaching is a permanent addition to the leadership development repertoire. Over the next few years, the right coaches will remain in the business, tighter talent-management connections will be established, and certain impact metrics will become widely adopted. Coaching has found its permanent position in the development landscape.

And finally, coaching has benefited greatly from the passionate and dedicated contributions of leaders, leadership development practitioners, and coaches. The field has been brought to life by these people, and by their organizations, which have embraced what coaching has to offer. We feel fortunate that we have had the opportunity to work with these amazing practitioners, and we thank them for their efforts in creating and growing the field of coaching.

Coaching Highlights

Coaching is not a temporary fad, but a permanent entrant into the development landscape. While the practice will continue to standardize, certification and government legislation are not predicted for the future. New forms of coaching, such as leader-as-coach, team coaching, and peer coaching are emerging. Developmental coaching—much longer and much deeper—is also gaining credence.

- **Guarantee it.** Increase accountability by tying coach pay to leader improvement. Assuming leaders follow the policies of the coaching engagement, it is thus possible to guarantee results.
- **Measure it.** Daily. Peer coaching involves partners measuring each others' goals every day. This one-to-one accountability greatly enhances focus and goal attainment.
- **Get tech savvy.** Online follow-up tools, simultaneous document editing, and video-assisted coaching all add great value to coaching interactions. Many such tools are free or at low cost.

Coaching Program Design Checklist

A copy of this document is available for download at www.executivecoaching 4results.com.

Establishing a successful coaching program requires thoughtful design as early as possible in the process. Recent coaching success stories, such as those featured in this book, began by carefully planning their coaching strategies from the outset. Today, many of these firms have documented successes with large numbers of senior executives.

The key questions to consider in establishing or enhancing a coaching program have been compiled into this one place, based on our research and many years of designing coaching programs with organizations. Even coaching initiatives that have been more ad hoc in nature can be steadily improved by thinking through and acting upon some of the questions presented here.

Link Coaching to Leadership Development and Talent Management

A coaching effort should be linked to a company's leadership development strategy (which ought to be linked to business strategy). Otherwise coaching may be too ad hoc and not necessarily moving leaders closer to organizational objectives. How will coaching fit within the leadership development strategy? What percent of a leader's development should come from coaching? And, how much coaching should be provided to different levels of leaders?

The leadership development strategy also identifies the competencies leaders need for future organizational success, and in turn, how coaching should support this. The purpose of coaching can then be identified (i.e., retain high potentials, accelerate transition, improve leadership capability).

Talent management systems identify which leaders are eligible for coaching and what type of development they will need. How will coaching be linked to the talent management approach (if any)? Which leaders should be eligible for coaching? How will coaching outcomes be tracked in the talent management system? Do all leaders in a particular level automatically receive coaching? Or do leaders engage with a coach at their own discretion?

Finally, if coaching is being used for performance problem employees, will that use continue? How will requests for performance issues be handled if coaching turns out not to be the right answer?

Culture and Leadership Support

Our research, not surprisingly, found that an organization's culture plays a major role in its support of people development and coaching. What are the organization's stated and subtle views toward people development? What is the history of coaching in the company? How is coaching perceived in the organization (for those high potential, high performers, or for those in trouble?) For non-friendly coaching cultures, find leaders willing to give it a try, secure a high profile executive sponsor, add coaching to existing training programs, provide coaches for new leaders, or even use coaching for those at the first-line supervisor level.

Senior leadership plays a pivotal role in shaping an organization's culture. What is the senior leadership's view on coaching? Do these leaders work with coaches? Do others know these leaders work with coaches? Are these leaders publicly supporting coaching? With nonsupportive leadership, identify a credible executive sponsor for the effort. Tell potential coachees they have been specially selected for the program. Discontinue the use of coaching for performance problem leaders and let some time elapse before starting a new program.

If a coaching program has not begun in earnest, selecting the right leaders to go first is important. They will serve as positive examples for others. Who are the right leaders to begin first (those well-regarded by the rest of the organization and willing to endorse coaching)? Collecting and publicizing testimonials from these leaders will carry great weight for other candidates.

Marketing/Communications

A coaching program will need some level of internal marketing to properly position the effort throughout the organization. What is the best approach to marketing the program? Consider such options as an internal Web site, marketing to worldwide leadership development and human resources, executive sponsor support, coachee testimonials, aggregated success data, etc. Alternatively, a more limited or exclusive program may not need a marketing effort at all.

Communicating the roles and responsibilities of all parties associating with coaching is also key. How will the executive be prepared for coaching? Will the executive know what coaching is about, and what role is expected of the executive? What about the local HR staff, or key stakeholders of the leader? The coachee's boss (call him or her the sponsor) is a major player and would benefit from focused communications clarifying his/her role as well.

Matching

Triaging coaching requests ensures that coaching is really the right intervention for a given request. Who will conduct this triage (i.e., HR, or leadership development) and how will it be done (i.e., phone interview, online request form)?

Research with leaders who have received coaching revealed the personal match between leaders and their coach to be an absolutely critical factor. How is matching to be made? Is the leader assigned a coach, does the leader select from two to three options, or will the leader choose a coach from a large list? Does the leader interview possible coach candidates, and if so, are interviews via phone or in person? Should the leader be encouraged to pick a coach of similar style/background (for camaraderie) or a vastly different coach (to challenge him or her)? Some organizations produce a guide or handbook for leaders to use to assist them in selecting a coach.

Once an assignment is underway, what is done to verify that the match is still a good one, and when is such verification done? Should leadership development or human resources check in with the leader? Or should a short survey be administered to measure the leader's satisfaction to date?

What process will be followed if negative feedback is obtained? Is the coach replaced immediately or given a chance to rectify? Does the problem lie with the coach or perhaps with the leader? (If another coach is assigned, will the same problems emerge?)

Instrumentation

Nearly all coaching begins with some sort of feedback process. How will feedback be collected (interviews, corporate leadership competency 360, off-the-shelf 360 tool)? If a coach has his or her own leadership tool or 360 instrument, can he or she use it? Determine who has access to these results as well.

What other instruments can be used? Can coaches use any instruments they recommend, or will there be limits? How much money can be spent on additional instruments, if any?

Assignment Activities

How long should assignments last? Do all leaders receive coaching for six months, for 12 months, or some other standard length of time? Should these lengths vary by leader or by level in the organization? Can leaders upgrade from shorter to longer lengths if desired? Who pays for coaching (the leader's budget, central corporate budget, or some combination)?

How often is coaching conducted? What is the expected mixture of face-to-face, telephone, and online coaching? Do coaches/leaders or the organization determine this mixture?

Organizations vary on the types of activities to be conducted during coaching; some outline exactly the steps and activities, whereas others allow coaches to use their discretion. Some of the many activities to be considered include action plan generation, reviewing an action plan with a manager, assessment tools, behavioral rehearsal/practice, leader following up with key stakeholders, coach following up with key stakeholders, coach locating resources (books, conferences) for leader, and follow-up mini surveys. Also, will coaches have enough time and budget to shadow the leader, observing him or her in various settings?

Many organizations require some filing of action plans. Will such filing be a part of the process? Where does the plan get filed, and who sees it? Is there a template plan that ought to be followed?

Finally, what happens when assignments conclude? Should coaching continue informally in a senior advisor capacity? If so, will the coach's time for this be reimbursed in some way?

Outcomes

A variety of metrics can be put into a coaching program. The first (Level one) is satisfaction. Is the leader satisfied with the coach? Will this satisfaction be measured, and, if so, how? Will human resources or leadership development check in with the leader from time to time? Or will there be some sort of automated survey process?

Did the leader make progress back on the job as a result of coaching (Level three)? This can be accomplished through a repeat 360 or a mini-survey (a very short 360 measuring improvement). An assessment from the manager of the leader being coached is another way to view this.

Level four measures the impact on the business, or the return on investment (ROI). Many organizations seek to measure ROI but find it difficult to quantify. Will there be an effort to obtain the ROI of coaching? If so, how? The most commonly attempted method is to ask the leader's assessment of business impact and to create a figure from this assessment. Another version looks at whether coached leaders are retained by the organization for a longer period of time than uncoached leaders, and to apply a dollar value to not losing the leader.

Internal Coaches

Coaching benefits can often be extended to more levels of management through the use of internal coaches. Some companies may use internal coaches exclusively if their culture is unique. Will internal coaches be used, and, if so, where? How will these coaches be trained? What are the boundaries of confidentiality for them?

The greatest challenge of internal coaches is time. Do they have enough time to do this job? Will they also have their traditional responsibilities, or is coaching their only requirement? Are internals viewed as credible and trustworthy in the organization?

Coach Sourcing

Locating high quality coaches is an ongoing challenge for the human resources and leadership development professional. How many coaches does your firm need, and where does it need them? Coaches can be found through full-service coaching vendors, coach referral networks, recommendations from other companies, professional associations, and the Web. Many coaches reach out to leadership development professionals and directly to the company's leaders as well.

Screening these coaches is another great challenge. What will be the key criteria to use in screening coaches? What will be the relative importance of such criteria as business experience (line and/or staff), coaching experience, industry experience, match to the organization's culture, ability to build rapport, advanced degree, location, cost, instrument certification, and coaching certification? What process will be used to screen the coaches (i.e., completing a form, interviews with corporate personnel, day long assessment process, accepting coaches from preferred vendors, etc.)?

Coach Community

Building a pool of coaches can represent a strong partnership between the organization and its coaches. Once coaches are accepted into the pool, will they receive an orientation? If so, is it held just one time, quarterly, virtually?

Coaches greatly appreciate ongoing communication with the firm and with each other. Will there be ongoing conference calls with the coaches, and if so, how often will they take place? What other information can be shared with the coaches (i.e., press releases, organizational restructuring, annual reports)? Will the firm host an annual (or some other periodical) forum with all coaches in the pool? Who pays for this event and for its associated travel expenses?

Logistical Considerations

Does purchasing/procurement need to be involved in the contracting process along the way? Will there be a formal contract and/or nondisclosure that coaches need to complete? If coaching is paid out of different budgets, is there a relatively easy way to establish these contracts internally?

How do coaches invoice for services, and how often? How are travel expenses handled (as part of the contract or as additional items)? What travel policy should coaches follow, and how will the prescribed policy be communicated to them? Do coaches have access to the company travel department? Can coaches receive access to the corporate intranet or receive entry badges at facilities?

Finally, an internal resource is generally needed to manage the coaching operation. Alternatively, external vendor(s) can handle these responsibilities. Who will play this role, and how much of their time will be required? How much information will be tracked, and how should this information be stored? Will a Coaching Management System be employed to oversee everything?

The worksheet on the following pages frames most of the preceeding considerations into a simple questionnaire that can be used to complete the design of the program. Although not all questions will have immediate answers, at least they should all be considered in the design or enhancement of a program.

Link to Leadership Development and Talent Management

How will coaching link to the leadership development strategy?	
What % of a leader's development will come from coaching?	
How much coaching is to be provided to different levels of leader?	
What is the main purpose of coaching (i.e., develop leaders, retain high potentials, accelerate transition, etc.)?	
How is coaching linked to the talent management system (if any)?	
Will the talent management system identify which leaders are eligible for coaching?	
Are coaching activities/outcomes to be tracked in the talent management system?	
Is coaching to be used for performance management problems? If not, how will performance management coaching requests be rerouted?	

Culture and Leadership Support

What is the culture's attitude toward development and coaching?	
What is the history of coaching in the organization?	
How is coaching perceived in the company (favorably, negatively)?	
Do senior leaders work with coaches? Do they publicly endorse coaching?	
If coaching has not yet begun, which leaders should be the first to go? (Consider those good role models first.)	
Is there a plan to collect testimonials from leaders to share with other prospective clients?	

Marketing/Communications

How will the program be marketed (if at all)? Consider: internal Web site marketing to worldwide leadership development and human resources, executive sponsor support, coachee testimonials, etc.	
Will there be a communication effort for all parties, to clarify their roles in the coaching process (i.e., coaching recipient, leader's manager, local HR, other key stakeholders)?	

Matching

How will matching be made? Are leaders given 2–3 options, do they select from a list, or is a coach simply assigned?	
Will there be a guide for leaders to assist them in selecting a coach?	
Do leaders interview coaches? If so, are interviews via phone or in person?	
Will there be a process to verify that the match was a good one (i.e., LD check-in with leader, short satisfaction survey)?	

Instrumentation

How will feedback be collected (interviews, off-the-shelf 360, customized 360)?	
Can coaches use any tools they recommend? Or are only certain tools approved for use in the organization? If so, which ones?	
How will additional tools be paid for? Will there be a budget?	

Assignment Activities

What are the assignment lengths? What is the expected mix of face-to-face/telephone/ online coaching?	
How often is coaching expected to occur? (Or is this up to the leader and coach?)	
Which activities (if any) are to be requisite parts of the coaching program (i.e., action plan generation, reviewing action plan with manager, assessment tools, behavioral rehearsal/practice, leader following up with key stakeholders, coach following up with key stakeholders, coach locating resources [(i.e., books, conferences)] for leader, follow-up mini surveys, shadowing, etc.)?	
Will there be an official method for filing action plans? Who sees these plans? Is there a standard template to use?	
How is coaching paid for? (Central LD budget? leader's budget? combination?)	
What happens when assignments finish? Is there some informal *senior advisor* role for the coach?	

Outcomes

Which outcome metrics will be used, and how will data be collected (i.e., leader self-assessment, boss assessment, repeat 360, mini 360)?	
Will leader satisfaction with coach be obtained? How and when?	
Is there an effort to measure return on investment? If so, how?	

Internal Coaches

Will internal coaches be used? If so, for what level(s) of leader?	
How are internal coaches trained? What are the criteria to become an internal coach?	
Do internal coaches have enough time to coach and carry out their other responsibilities?	
What are the confidentiality boundaries for internal coaches?	

Coach Sourcing

How many coaches are required, and where?	
How will coaches be found (current vendors, referral networks, other company recommendations, professional associations, web, coaches who contact your leaders or yourself)?	
What criteria will be used to screen coaches (i.e., business experience [(line and/or staff)], coaching experience, industry experience, match the organization's culture, ability to build rapport, advanced degree, location, cost, instrument certification, and coaching certification)?	
How will coaches be screened (completing a form, interviews with corporate personnel, daylong assessment process, accepting coaches from preferred vendors)?	

Coach Community

How will coaches be oriented to the organization?	
What ongoing communication efforts will be used (quarterly conference calls, press releases, organization announcements, etc.)?	
Will there be a regular gathering of coaches? How often, and who pays for this?	

Logistical Considerations

Does purchasing need to be involved in the contracting with coaches and coaching providers? What about a nondisclosure agreement? Is there an easy way to open a coaching contract (especially if coaching is paid for by different budgets)?	
How do coaches invoice for services and how often?	
What travel policies should coaches follow? Do coaches have access to a company travel department?	
Can coaches receive access to corporate intranet or entry badges for facilities?	
Is there an internal resource to manage all coaching activities and/or an external vendor to do the same?	
What information should this resource track, how will it be stored, and who will have access to this information?	

Afterword

The Call to Coaching

Richard J. Leider

People come to coaching for many different reasons, but the bottom line is change. In the accelerating environment of perpetual change, executives who cannot manage the discontinuities of their own lives and careers will not produce great results no matter how good their technical skills or leadership capacities.

We all know that change has become the most dependable reality in our lives and leadership. But that was not true for most of the twentieth century. That world seemed fairly certain and dependable, so our lives and our leadership took on those dimensions.

Today, the most probable scenario for the future is that change will accelerate steadily in both speed and in the number of life dimensions affected. Although we're not the first human beings to face the breakdowns and breakthroughs of constant change, the technological and global aspects of our situations are new. So our lives and our leadership must take on these new dimensions.

Executives today need to develop their own personal expression of leadership, based on integrity and authenticity. They must learn how to embody leadership. The leadership demand recognizes that expertise alone is not enough. Instead, leadership demands both competency and character. Coaches help executives discover the advantages of both competence and character. Coaches are both change agents and constants agents. They help people see what needs to change and what needs to remain constant or unchanging.

The more the world around us is in flux, the more we must be certain about what matters in our lives: the purpose, the values, the ethics that don't change. When the macrosystems in our world are in considerable flux, as they are today, the microsystems in our lives, the constants, rise in importance. A coach can show how this happens.

Today, as this wise book shows us, the field of coaching is emerging from its adolescence, finding its voice, taking a stand. Those of us who have pioneered the training of coaches and coached executives ourselves know the extraordinary impact coaching can have on people's lives and leadership. The call to coaching is the satisfaction that effective coaches take in seeing their clients let go of old practices and begin to follow new practices that give them strength to succeed in the changing situations they find themselves. That the coaching field itself continues to grow at an exponential rate is a tribute to the human need to grow and change.

The highest calling of coaches today is to become guides to a transient world, including transient corporate cultures. Leading-edge coaches model the future because they are willing to invent, design it, and insist on it. Effective coaches recognize that most executives use only a fraction of their potential to lead, and that the challenges faced by today's organizations require the full development and expression of the whole person. True leaders must develop all facets of their potential in order to lead, not just the narrow few needed to manage.

As predictability and stability give way to uncertainty and worry, executives are scrambling to find resources to help them look for shifting advantages within their ultracompetitive working worlds. Coaches fill some of the need. Coaches are catalysts for both change and constants. Most important, effective coaches can help executives anticipate and work through change with energy, purpose, and hope.

A coach may be one of our best investments for the future. Whether you are a coach, a leader, or both, a study of this book will be an equally wise investment. Coaches are strong, emerging resources. The time to use them wisely is now. By 2020, when a new type of purposeful leadership will probably have matured, we will observe our coaching approach to executive development and wonder how it could have been otherwise.

Notes

Frontmatter

1. Goldsmith & Morgan, "Leadership Is a Contact Sport," *Strategy + Business* (2004, Fall): 71–79.
2. Contact: Executive Development Associates, www.executivedevelopment.com.
3. Contact: Executive Development Associates, www.executivedevelopment.com.

Introduction

1. International Coach Federation. http://www.coachfederation.org
2. Sherman & Freas, "The Wild West of Executive Coaching," *Harvard Business Review* (2004, November).
3. As reported by Dingfelder, Sadie. "Post Grad Growth Area: Executive Coaching." gradPSYCH, (2006, November): 4:4.
4. As reported by the International Coach Federation. http://www.coachfederation. org.uk/research_and_publications/coaching_research.phtml

Chapter 1

1. Encyclopedia Britannica Online. http://www.britannica.com/ebc/article-9361016
2. O'Neil, Mary Beth. *Executive Coaching with Backbone and Heart: A Systems Approach to Engaging Leaders with Their Challenges* (San Francisco: Jossey-Bass, 2000).
3. Dotlich, D. & Cairo, P. *Action Coaching: How to Leverage Individual Performance for Company Success* (San Francisco: Jossey-Bass, 1999).
4. Kilberg, R. *Executive Coaching: Developing Managerial Wisdom in a World of Chaos* (Washington, DC: American Psychological Association, 2000).
5. Wikipedia. www.wikipedia.com

6. Watkins, M. *The First 90 Days: Critical Success Strategies for New Leaders at All Levels.* (Cambridge, MA: Harvard Business School Press, 2003).

Chapter 3

1. One of the many sources for this standard in the industry comes from Sweetman, Ulrich, and Smallwood. *Developing a Leadership Strategy.* Posted online at http://clomedia.com/content/templates/clo_article.asp?articleid=1641&zoneid=25
2. Contact: Executive Development Associates at www.executivedevelopment.com

Chapter 4

1. Goldsmith & Morgan, "Leadership Is a Contact Sport." *Strategy + Business* (2004, Fall): 71–79.

Chapter 8

1. See MetrixGlobal at www.metrixglobal.com
2. "Executive Coaching Yields Return on Investment of Almost Six Times Its Cost, Says Study." *Business Wire*, January 4, 2001.

Chapter 11

1. Richard Leider in July 2005 Minneapolis workshop.

Chapter 12

1. www.ifollowthrough.com
2. Sherman & Freas, "The Wild West of Executive Coaching," *Harvard Business Review* (2004, November).
3. Robert Reich in speech at Linkage's Global Institute for Leadership Development, (Palm Springs, CA: October 2006).

About the Authors

Brian O. Underhill, Ph.D.

Brian O. Underhill, Ph.D., is an industry-recognized expert in the design and management of global executive coaching implementations.

Brian is the Founder of CoachSource. He oversees worldwide coaching operations through a pool of over 600 leadership coaches. His executive coaching work helps executives achieve positive, measurable, long-term change in leadership behavior.

Brian is the engagement leader for the High-Impact Executive Coaching research study. His most recent article on Agilent Technologies' coaching program appears in *Coaching for Leadership*, second edition, (Pfeiffer: 2006) and *Best Practices in Leadership Development and Organization Change* (Pfeiffer: 2005). He is a regular speaker at The Conference Board, Linkage, ASTD New York and LA, HRPS New York, PCMA and other industry events.

Brian's clients include Agilent Technologies, AT&T, CalPERS, Dell, Johnson & Johnson, Motorola, and Sony. His nonprofit work has benefited the Drucker Foundation, St. Vincent de Paul Village, and the Union Rescue Mission.

Brian has a Ph.D. in organizational psychology from the California School of Professional Psychology, and a psychology degree from the University of Southern California.

Brian lives near Silicon Valley with his wife Lisa and children Kaitlyn and Evan. He is an avid soccer player and musician. He can be reached at: brian@coach-source.com or www.coach-source.com.

Kimcee McAnally, Ph.D.

Dr. McAnally's background includes over 20 years working in or consulting for businesses in the areas of strategy development, leadership development, executive coaching, training and education, and change management. She holds a B.A. in psychology and a master's and Ph.D. in organizational psychology.

Her consulting practice includes developing executive coaching and leadership development programs; planning and designing transition strategies; facilitating workshops and strategy sessions; developing training and education programs; company culture change; designing organizational and employee assessments; creating new organizational structures, roles, and responsibilities; communication planning and strategies; improving group processes; and transitions for implementation of new processes and technology in companies. Dr. McAnally also operates a research organization providing industry shared-research, directed-research, and thought-leadership. Her research background includes academic research, practical industry-wide studies, and written reports, articles, and publications.

Dr. McAnally's client list includes large and small companies representing retail, healthcare, grocery, and manufacturing industries. Her clients include American Eagle Outfitters, Babycenter.com, Barnes & Noble Booksellers, eToys, Dockers Khaki's, Hallmark Specialty Retail Group, HealthCare Partners, JC Penney, Jos. A Bank, Limited Inc., Neiman Marcus, Nordstrom, Party City, Rockwell International, Sears Canada, Sony Electronics, Teleflora, TJMaxx, Victoria's Secret Direct, and Wal-Mart. Kimcee can be reached at Kimcee@coach-source.com.

John Jay Koriath, Ph.D.

Dr. Koriath is a psychologist with a multidisciplinary career.

He is President of Full Circle Learning, Inc. and Vice President, Leadership Through Personal Development at ExecutiveNetworks, Inc. where has helped to create and deliver a community of practice networking experience to leaders of Fortune 1000 companies. John has held various positions with Executive Development Associates, Inc., and was VP of Research directing the seminal research study this book presents.

John is drawn to projects, people, and relationships that seek to bring positive change to twenty-first century living. He approaches his work with a diverse set of skills and experiences gathered in a career as an educator, scientist, and therapist.

John is a cofounder of the Turtle Island Project, a nonprofit organization whose programs integrate principles of mind and body through the teachings of Native American rituals and ceremonies. John is a student and instructor in the martial art of Aikido.

John also served for ten years on the faculty of Arizona State University, where he taught in the field of psychology. During that time he conducted psychophysiological research, in part as the Flinn Foundation Fellow for Cardiovascular Research.

Dr. Koriath published a variety of articles and book chapters while in academia. More recently his chapter, "Using Communities of Practice to Extend Learning beyond Classroom Walls," was in *The Future of Executive Development*, James F. Bolt, ed., 2005, Executive Development Associates, Inc. He also co-authored *High-Impact Executive Coaching*, research conducted with Executive Development Associates, Inc. in 2005.

About the Contributors

Kimberly Arnold

Kimberly Arnold currently works for Dell, Inc., where she manages organizational development for Dell's largest sales segment. She works directly with the leadership team to help drive change, grow leaders, and create impactful talent management process. She sees executive coaching as a critical and valuable part of developing strong sales leaders. In her prior Dell role, she managed their global executive coaching network and the partnership with their external coaching vendor. Before joining Dell in 2004, she was VP of Organizational Development for one of JPMorgan Chase's global business segments. With over 18 years' experience as an OD consultant, Kimberly uses executive coaches not only to coach executives, but also as OD partners who offer unique perspectives on the climate of the leadership. Kim and her husband John have a 10-year-old son Taylor and live in Austin Texas. In addition to enjoying amazing meals at home, prepared by her husband John, who is a Personal Chef, they like to spend weekends waterskiing and tubing with friends on Austin's beautiful Lake Travis.

Carol Braddick

Carol Braddick is an executive coach and consultant working primarily in the UK and the U.S. She and the associates in her business, Graham Braddick Partnership, design and deliver practical coaching and development programs to help executives and teams perform beyond past successes. Carol has been immersed in researching, writing, and speaking about company practices in coaching for several years. Carol has a bachelor's degree in Linguistics (Pomona College) and an MBA in Finance (NYU). Originally from New York, Carol has also lived and worked in Latin America. She, her British significant other, and their assorted pets live in a tiny village north of London with ample opportunities to step outside the world of coaching and enjoy countryside adventures and surprises. She can be reached through Graham Braddick Partnership, by telephone: 44(0)1371 811 533; mobile: 44(0)7836 684 785; or by e-mail at carol@carolbraddick.com.

Sue Brown

Sue J. Brown is Managing Partner of SJ Brown & Associates, a Houston, Texas-based executive coaching firm. During her career she has coached hundreds of leaders in Fortune 500 firms in the energy and technology industry to excel in their careers and guide their organizations to greater success. Sue believes that development is an essential part of both our business and personal lives. Her doctoral degree in executive leadership is from George Washington University in Washington, D. C. She may be contacted through www.sjbrownandassoc.com.

Mary Wayne Bush

Mary Wayne Bush is the Director of Research for The Foundation of Coaching. She is on the editorial board of the *International Journal of Coaching in Organizations*. Mary Wayne holds a master's degree from Yale University and a doctorate in Organizational Change from Pepperdine University. She works as a consulting strategic planner with Raytheon Missile Systems. She can be reached at marywayne@earthlink.net.

Kim Deutsch and Elaine Roberts

Elaine Roberts is the director of corporate human resources and people development for the Progressive Group of Insurance Companies. Kim Zitko Deutsch is the manager of People Development. They have worked together for six years, and they coauthored their contribution to this book. Elaine, Kim, and the people development team analyze, design, and develop selection, assessment, survey, leadership, and professional development processes and products impacting the span of the employee experience. Elaine and Kim view coaching as a culturally significant interaction yielding both personal and professional gains. Each has been coached at various points in her life, and each believes in the value of perpetuating this process of growth and development by coaching others.

Elaine holds a B.S. in management and has spent her 21-year career with Progressive. Kim has a B.S. in journalism and an MBA in marketing. She began her career as a consultant with Accenture where she worked for eight years, joining Progressive in 2001.

Susan Diamond

Susan Diamond is retained by The Conference Board to be Program Director, choosing speakers for its seminars and forums on executive coaching. She is chief learning officer and vice president of facilitation of the Women Presidents' Organization, which connects top women entrepreneurs in professionally facilitated peer advisory groups composed of company presidents. As an executive coach for 15 years, she has built a solid reputation in Fortune 500 companies for helping leaders develop "executive presence" and build on strengths found in diversity. Susan is a master certified teacher of Marshall Goldsmith's behavioral coaching methodology, and she holds a graduate degree in organizational psychology from Columbia University Teachers College and an undergraduate degree from Wellesley College. Her point of view regarding the approach and value of coaching was formed as a teenager, coaching and being coached in baton, 4-H, and student leadership in the farm community of Worland, Wyoming. Her commitment was further formed through her husband's football experience at Harvard, her daughter's swimming career at The Peddie School, and the development of her son's leadership capabilities at the United States Naval Academy at Annapolis—which is to say that even the best raw talent needs proper support and inspired coaching to reach the highest levels of performance. Susan believes coaching will become even more necessary and prevalent as companies grapple with the complexities of globalization.

Margaret L. Durr

Dr. Margaret L. Durr is the senior executive development consultant/coach at Wal-Mart Stores, Inc., for the officers of the executive committee as well as for those in the international, global procurement, and people divisions of the company. Margaret joined Wal-Mart in February 2005. Prior to joining Wal-Mart, she managed the testing and assessment program for Safeway, Inc. In addition, she worked for ACT as an Industrial/Organizational Psychologist, with clients such as Sunbeam, Neutrogena, GE Plastics, Bombardier, Corning, and Anheuser-Busch. Her prior experiences also include serving as director of workplace literacy at Valmont Industries, as the wage and salary administrator at Bergan Mercy Medical Center, and as adjunct faculty at both the university and community college levels. She believes in continuous learning, sharing knowledge, and taking a research perspective when pursuing our understanding of human behavior and the many individual differences within it. Executive coaching affords us the opportunity to help those in a position to "change the world," given their status and position therein.

Harris Ginsberg

Harris Ginsberg designs and deploys solutions to strengthen leadership and organizational capability, and to maximize the effectiveness of learning and development, and of executive coaching. In the corporate world as well as in the broader landscape of life, personal learning and growth enable us to gain mastery and experience deep awareness of our capability and potential. Learning allows us to navigate the twists and turns of life and rebound from disappointments or celebrate our successes. Currently director, organization development at Chemtura, Dr. Ginsberg is establishing talent development processes to support goals for revenue growth, market share, and leadership in the specialty chemical industry. In addition, Dr. Ginsberg is an adjunct assistant Professor at the Wagner School for Public Service at New York University. Formerly director of Global Executive and Organization Capability at IBM, he consulted with senior executives on applying leadership competencies to business results. He has held leadership roles in training and development at a variety of industries (JPMorgan Chase, Colgate Palmolive, Citibank, and Technicon). Prior to his corporate career, Dr. Ginsberg worked as a psychologist in private practice and at Pace University's Counseling Center, helping people overcome obstacles to their personal success. Dr. Ginsberg earned a B.S. in psychology at Union College (Schenectady), an M.Ed. in counseling at the University of Hartford, and a Ph.D. in counseling psychology at the University of Pennsylvania, with a minor in organizational behavior at the Wharton School. Dr. Ginsberg has taught at the Choate Rosemary Hall School, University of Delaware, Mercy College, and Pace University in New York.

Dr. Ginsberg is a licensed psychologist in New York State and a member of the American Psychological Association. He is a member of the Conference Board's advisory board on executive coaching.

Heidi M. Glickman

Heidi M. Glickman, Ph.D., SPHR, is assistant vice president of leadership development at MassMutual Financial Group. Joining Mass Mutual in January 2007, she is responsible for succession planning and executive development. Prior to joining MassMutual, she grew and led the executive development function at Wal-Mart Stores, Inc., for more than four years. Her prior experiences include consultant, specializing in leadership development, and roles in higher education administration. Heidi believes coaching is a key component of any leadership development strategy, effectively supporting leaders in accelerating personal learning and development, applying new skills, gaining critical feedback, and growing personal effectiveness.

Marshall Goldsmith

Marshall Goldsmith is a world authority on helping successful leaders achieve positive, lasting change in behavior: for themselves, for their people, and for their teams. Dr. Goldsmith is the author or coeditor of 22 books, including *What Got You Here Won't Get You There*, which has been ranked as America's #1 best-selling business book in the *Wall Street Journal*. Marshall is one of the few executive advisors who have been asked to work with over 80 CEOs and their management teams. He was recognized by *Forbes* as one of the five most-respected executive coaches, by the *Economist* as one of three most credible executive advisors in the new era of business, and by *Fast Company* as America's pre-eminent executive coach.

Bob Gregory

As talent management and learning manager in BP's North America Gas Strategic Performance Unit, Bob is responsible for a wide range of activities around the development of talent and succession planning for the future of one of BP's key resources. Bob's career has been marked and shaped by holding roles around the development of individuals and has gravitated to a particular emphasis on leadership development. Prior to BP, other positions have included public sector, not-for-profit organizations, and corporate positions. Bob has held a professorship of behavioral sciences and leadership, and various other behavioral scientist positions in the Air Force; he has been an SVP of learning and development in banking, and the director of the Center for Creative Leadership's San Diego branch.

With an undergraduate degree in Biology, a Master's in Counseling, and a Doctorate in Psychology, Bob finds that his interests have always been around wonderment and discovery of the science and application of science to human behavior, and how those processes fit together to impact societies—large and small. "Graduating" into leadership development and working with "high-normals" in the corporate sector has led to his exploration of how those in leadership positions can best be equipped—tools and methodologies—to improve business performance, ultimately, to the improvement of societal institutions. Increasingly he has been involved with the techniques of coaching and the growing body of evidence supporting it, and how and when to effectively utilize executive coaching (as well as the limitations of) gained interest. This interest and Bob's involvement in the selection and assessment of coaches and coaching have led him to take a keen interest in the appropriate use of coaching. Used suitably, coaching can be one of the most important and key tools to be judiciously applied for improving the performance of executives—not only in the corporate sector, but in all sectors of society.

William Hodgetts

William Hodgetts is an experienced, senior executive coach who brings an extensive knowledge of leadership development, executive assessment, behavioral science and family business to his work with CEOs and other senior leaders. Bill is currently Vice President of Leadership & Executive Development at Fidelity Investments, where his responsibilities include providing executive coaching, developmental assessments, and other learning resources to senior executives. Bill also oversees executive coaching company-wide, and maintains an extensive referral network of coaching and other development resources. Bill is a founding Board member of The Executive Coaching Forum, an organization devoted to establishing and promoting the highest standards of professional and ethical practice for the field of executive coaching. He has presented frequently at national conferences on executive coaching and leadership developemnt, and is author of "Using Executive Coaching in Organizations: What Can Go Wrong (And How to Prevent It)," in Executive Coaching, Catherine Fitzgerald, editor, Davies Black, Fall 2001; also co-author (with Jane Hodgetts) of "Finding Sanctuary in Post-Modern Life," from The Career is Dead, edited by Douglas T. Hall, Jossey-Bass, 1996. Bill holds an Ed.D. in human development and psychology from Harvard University, and a B.A. in government from Cornell University.

Alison Hu

Alison Hu is the leadership coaching global program manager in global learning and leadership development at Agilent Technologies in Santa Clara, California. She holds a BS and MS in Electrical Engineering and an MS in Industrial Engineering & Engineering Management, all from Stanford University. Alison began her career at Agilent as a manufacturing engineer and, with the help of several mentors, moved into training and leadership development. Her passion is helping others find and express their leadership voice and achieve their dreams.

Sam Humphrey

Sam Humphrey from Unilever works through a program called GRIT. The program's premise is to support leaders and their teams to increase their leadership impact at a cognitive, emotional, and behavioral level. Her career path has been heavily influenced by asking and being asked great questions and by giving or receiving brave and meaningful feedback. Sam values authenticity and integrity in herself and others, and her executive coaching is all about meaning—making to support and enable a leader make a constructive impact in the world, regardless of whether this is at a global level or one to one. She believes executive coaching can add tremendous value to an individual's personal leadership journey, and can see this continuing for some time to come.

Barbara Kenny

Barb Kenny is Senior OD specialist in Dell's Global Talent Management team. In this role, she manages Dell's global executive coaching network and is responsible for designing and implementing global leadership and executive development initiatives.

Prior to Dell, Barb was a Manager in Cap Gemini, Ernst & Young's Organization Transformation practice, where she led a variety of global change initiatives for Fortune 500 companies in the telecommunications, automotive, and high-tech industries. She has over 17 years of human resources and OD experience which she uses to help global organizations maximize their return on talent management investments and "create the space" needed to truly accelerate development of leaders at all levels of an organization.

Anthony I. Lamera

Anthony I. Lamera has been with CalPERS Human Resources—all staff training and development—since 1999. Anthony is the coordinator for CalPERS Succession Planning & Workforce Management program. Anthony administrates the biennial 360 multi-rater feedback and coaching process and conducts the leadership skills assessment process for mid-level managers to executive staff. Anthony feels that the greatest legacy a leader can leave behind is a well-prepared and capable successor.

Christine Landon

Christine Landon is currently the senior director of executive and next generation leadership development at Agilent Technologies in Santa Clara, California. She has over 25 years of experience in the area of leadership and executive development, holding other positions at Hewlett Packard in human resources, change management, and organization strategy and effectiveness. She also held various positions in UC Berkeley's MBA program for executives in the Haas School of Business. Christine holds both an MBA and a BS in Psychology from UC Berkeley. She has a passion for development, both at work and in her community, and she is committed to helping leaders grow, believing the opportunity to work with a coach one on one has been invaluable to the executives she supports.

Richard Leider

Ranked by *Forbes* as one of the Top Five most-respected coaches, Richard Leider is a best-selling author with thirty years' experience in coaching people to live and work on purpose. As founder and chairman of the Inventure Group, he is an internationally recognized speaker who works with many leading organizations such as 3M, Boeing, American Express, Pfizer, and the Mayo Clinic. As a leader in executive development, Richard has taught over 100,000 executives from 50 corporations worldwide. He is the author of seven books, including three best-sellers, and his work has been translated into 17 languages. *Repacking Your Bags* and *The Power of Purpose* are considered classics in the personal development field. His newest book, *Claiming Your Place at the Fire*, has been touted as the defining book on the new retirement. As a commentator on life transitions, Richard has been published in the *Wall Street Journal*, *The New York Times*, and *USA Today*, and he has appeared as a guest on television and public radio. A nationally certified master career counselor, Richard also holds a Master's Degree in counseling and is a senior fellow at the University of Minnesota's Center for Spirituality and Healing. He consistently receives the highest marks as an educator in the Global Learning Resource Network of Duke Corporate Education, and he is an adjunct faculty member at the University of Minnesota Carlson School's Executive Development Center. Along with his professional pursuits, Richard has led annual Inventure Expedition walking safaris in East Africa for over 20 years. His work has received recognition from the Bush Foundation, from which he was awarded a Bush Fellowship to study "purposeful aging." Believing passionately that each of us is born with a purpose, he is dedicated to coaching people to discover their own power of purpose.

Janet Matts

Janet is an executive coach, OD and leadership development consultant, and, most recently, director, executive assessment and coaching, for Johnson and Johnson in New Brunswick, New Jersey, responsible for creating the infrastructure for the executive coaching process for the corporation. In her 21 years with the company, her work has included coaching and consulting with a variety of senior executives, teams, and others in the organization in the areas of leadership, organizational development, strategy, change, new product development, transitions, 360° feedback, and globalization. Her first career in the field of education included a Peace Corps assignment starting one of the country's first schools for mentally handicapped children in Nairobi, Kenya. Her career at Johnson & Johnson has drawn upon her continued multicultural and multinational experiences, and it has included serving as the EarthWatch Volunteer in 2001, when she spent seven weeks working in the slums of Chennai, India, on a maternal and child healthcare project. In each of these experiences and in the work in the corporation, there has always been a theme around human potential and coaching to that potential. "In all my work and life I focus on the building of a sustainable community to allow for significant breakthroughs. Executive coaching is about that community of coaches who serve as change agents, working with leaders who have the opportunity to create the change and carry that change process in the communities we call organizations. Changes in this system create the sustainable differences in our work, in our world. Coaches need to be systemic thinkers, seeing integration and prioritization as critical elements to sustain the needed changes in our global world." Janet earned an M.A. in education from Columbia University in New York and a B.A. in education/psychology at Moravian College in Pennsylvania. Janet also holds a supervisory certification in educational administration from Rutgers University, and she is a graduate of the Hudson Institute of Santa Barbara, California, holding a coaching credential.

Mary O'Hara

Mary O'Hara joined TD Bank Financial Group as Senior Vice President, Organization Development, Human Resources, in August 2006. Mary is responsible for overseeing TD's Organization Development functions including Talent Management, Staffing, Performance Management, Organizational Design, Learning and Development, and HR Research & Measurement.

Over the past 10 years prior to joining TD, Mary held increasingly senior roles in Human Resources at Bell Canada Enterprises where she led their award-winning people development practice. She has also held a number of HR management positions for the Canadian operations of two diverse international organizations.

Mary obtained her Certified Human Resources Professional designation in 1994. She has studied at the University of Southern California, Queen's University, and the Rotman School of Management in the areas of Advanced Telecommunications Management, Marketing, and Change Management.

She is an active member of The Financial Institutions Advisory Council, The Chang School, Ryerson University. Mary is a guest speaker at various HR conferences and seminars where she shares her experience, expertise, and insights.

Mary resides in Oakville with her husband and two children.

Kristin Olsen

Kristin Olsen works for Thrivent Financial for Lutherans in the enterprise talent office. She describes her team's purpose as helping leaders make better decisions about talent, and helping individuals refine and develop their careers. She has worked in human resource development for 17 years, completing her MA in that area in 2003. Kristin derives great personal fulfillment from helping people grow and develop. Early on, she worked in the presentation of management development programs, and she is now a development coach for high-potential employees. Being given the opportunity to help others discover their vocational strengths is extremely rewarding for her. She believes many people need help articulating and planning their careers and can thrive with coaching and direction. She also sees executive coaching as a way to link the needs of the organization with those of individuals. It is frequently the missing leadership competency within organizations that, if present, can become a competitive advantage.

Kenneth J. Rediker, Ph.D.

Ken Rediker, Ph.D., is director, management development, for Saudi Aramco (www.saudiaramco.com), and he works in the company's corporate headquarters in Dhahran, Saudi Arabia. In this role Ken provides leadership for corporate processes focused on the identification, development, and selection of individuals for top 200 positions in the company. Ken's life and career path have both been full of unexpected turns and events, which have been significant sources of the most challenging and rewarding parts of his life. His time with Saudi Aramco is a prime example. Ken values hard work and hard play, and he takes pleasure in working with individuals who are self-motivated and have divergent points of views on developing leaders and living a full life. Ken sees coaching as a potentially valuable process that can accelerate development in focused areas of need or interest. He expects that coaching will be viewed in the future as one type of intervention that can be of particular relevance to the development of executives if they are willing to engage in honest reflection about the feedback they receive during the coaching process and can integrate this with their own personal desires and professional aspirations.

Pat Santillanes

Pat Santillanes is the assistant chief of CalPERS human resources, and he provides leadership and direction to a number of HR-related functions. Pat provided continuity and support for the 360-degree multi-rater leadership feedback and coaching process established in 1996, and he has been responsible for augmenting the program with a Web-based tool to ensure that leaders follow through with their individual development goals. Pat believes that continuous learning is a minimum requirement for personal development, and that the 360° process and external coaching are truly best practices that contribute to CalPERS's overall success.

Stephen E. Sass

Stephen E. Sass is the President of Sass & Associates, Inc., a virtual professional services firm that specializes in helping individuals and organizations improve their "business performance." He started this organization in 1997 after 28 years in IBM Customer Service and Education and 4 at KPMG, LLP where he led a transformation of the learning organization in support of the firm's strategy. As the day-to-day project leader for the Global Coaching contract with Dell Computer, Steve helps to maximize the benefits that Dell seeks from Executive Coaching. "Working with these intelligent, talented leaders and helping to make a difference in their leadership capabilities, especially as they lead individuals and teams, is a real joy in my life." Dell and other companies he works with see Executive Coaching as a very personal, targeted, and efficient way to address development targets of good leaders who want to get even better.

Lori Severson

Lori Severson is a coach and consultant for leaders in business, with 20 years of experience managing and developing people in Fortune 500 companies including Intel, GE, and Honeywell. Lori holds an M.A. in organizational communication and is a certified coach through the Newfield Network School of Coaching. Her primary emphasis is on creating leaders who lead from their core purpose, using a "3D" process in which clients discover, design, and develop themselves to new levels of leadership. She encourages leaders to be courageous, authentic, and passionate for their own and their company's purpose. Wouldn't we all like to be doing more meaningful work? Keen on driving a deeper sense of value for the people side of business, her bias is that leaders today affect the world and, as such, need to be bottom-line focused *and beyond*. She believes that coaching is unlike any other development process in that it serves as a catalyst for significant change and growth for already successful leaders. *Lori believes you can make a difference one conversation at a time!*

Deborah Swanson

Debby Swanson is national director of talent & organizational development at Sony Electronics, Inc. She is responsible for strategic learning and leadership development for executives, high potential managers, and leaders at all levels. She approaches development holistically with broad outcomes that include alignment and collaboration across silos, culture change, enhanced understanding of industry and markets, and building individual and organizational capability. Debby's passion has always been as a pathfinder to encourage others to see and achieve their potential in all areas of life, regardless of the challenges or circumstances. She provides 360° feedback and executive coaching for emerging and high-potential leaders, those in transition to a new role. She is a mentor for senior women in other organizations. In this time of increasing complexity and rapid change, Debby believes that an executive coach can help any executive greatly enhance his or her effectiveness and ability to navigate unchartered courses.

Zeynep Tozum

Zeynep is an executive performance coach who works with executives and business teams around the world. She sees coaching as her way of contributing to her and other people's growth, encouraging them to stretch and so to bring out their best, for remarkable results. She believes human potential is endless when people aspire to go beyond their existing limitations. Zeynep was with Unilever for more than 20 years in roles related to change management, marketing, business restructuring, and cost-management projects. She later became vice president, performance development, supporting businesses around the world. In February 2006, she set up her own practice, FARBEYOND, in the field of organizational transformation for performance development. Zeynep holds BA and MA degrees in economics. She can be reached through zeynep.tozum@farbeyondconsulting.com or www.farbeyondconsulting.com.

Janet Weakland

Janet (Jan) M. Weakland is the Houston challenge manager for the exploration and production segment within BP, where she manages a competency-based, early development program for all disciplines of college graduate new hires. Early in her career, Jan began a self-transformation journey, in which she discovered the value of life-long learning and personal growth, and she developed the enthusiasm to help others in their transformational journeys. Jan's passion and commitment to helping others by enhancing their professional and personal growth has led her down a career path of more than 20 years in learning and organizational development. Through her transformational journey, Jan has experienced firsthand the value of executive coaching, both by being coached and by coaching others. She believes that executive coaching inspires people to unlock their hidden potentials and maximize performance at both the individual and organizational levels, and that the demand for executive coaching will only increase due to the great pressure in the workplace for immediate results.

Kevin Wilde

As VP-CLO, Kevin Wilde leads the corporate organization effectiveness team at General Mills, Inc. His major responsibilities center around stewardship of core people and organization development systems, the General Mills Leadership Institute, and business consulting. His work has been recognized by *Training Magazine*'s Top 100 award, *Chief Executive Magazine*'s Top 20 for leadership development, and *Chief Learning Officer Magazine*'s Gold Award for leading business change. Prior to joining General Mills, Kevin was a seventeen-year veteran of General Electric. He served in two high-growth divisions and also in two corporate roles, managing global leadership development at the Crotonville Education Center and leading corporate WorkOut consulting. Kevin's calling is to connect people to their potential through learning, and he believes executive coaching can be a great way to do this. He sees the biggest change in executive education to be that there is a more sophisticated customer of coaching services and, therefore, a need for a stronger executive coaching practice.

Author Company Affiliations

CoachSource

Brian O. Underhill, Ph.D. is Founder and CEO of CoachSource. Brian launched CoachSource in 2006 to focus solely on leadership coaching. Our roots originate from Alliance for Strategic Leadership (A4SL) and Keilty Goldsmith & Company. The company manages some of the largest global leadership coach engagements. CoachSource features a network of over 600 leadership coaches around the world. (408) 779-9059, brian@coach-source.com, www.coach-source.com.

Claris Solutions

Kimcee McAnally, Ph.D. is a partner with Claris Solutions, a management consulting firm established to help companies improve their performance, customer service, and bottom line. The partnership is organized around a peer model, which we believe is the very best way to deliver insightful solutions, real results, with the highest payback, using the most experienced practitioners. We offer services including leadership development and executive coaching, business process improvement, project management, and change management. (760) 846-0461, kimcee@coach-source.com or Kimcee@claris-solutions.com.

Full Circle Learning

John Jay Koriath, Ph.D is President and CEO of Full Circle Learning, Inc., a company whose activities focus on developing *leadership through personal development*. Through coaching, mentoring, consulting, and powerful, custom designed workshops, Full Circle Learning guides individuals, leaders, and organizations committed to *sustaining soul in everyday life*. (206) 567-5394, jjk@fullc.com, www.fullcirclelearning.com.

Executive Development Associates

Executive Development Associates (EDA) is a leader in creating custom-designed executive development strategies, systems and programs that help organizations build the capabilities needed to achieve their strategic objectives and ensure that the organization's executive talent becomes a clear competitive advantage. EDA has world renowned experts in custom-designed programs, executive assessments, talent management technology and executive coaching. (866) EXEC DEV, EDA@executivedevelopment.com, www.executivedevelopment.com

Index

Page number followed by *f* or *t* indicates figure or table.

Berrett–Koehler
Publishers

Berrett-Koehler is an independent publisher dedicated to an ambitious mission: *Creating a World That Works for All*.

We believe that to truly create a better world, action is needed at all levels—individual, organizational, and societal. At the individual level, our publications help people align their lives with their values and with their aspirations for a better world. At the organizational level, our publications promote progressive leadership and management practices, socially responsible approaches to business, and humane and effective organizations. At the societal level, our publications advance social and economic justice, shared prosperity, sustainability, and new solutions to national and global issues.

A major theme of our publications is "Opening Up New Space." Berrett-Koehler titles challenge conventional thinking, introduce new ideas, and foster positive change. Their common quest is changing the underlying beliefs, mindsets, institutions, and structures that keep generating the same cycles of problems, no matter who our leaders are or what improvement programs we adopt.

We strive to practice what we preach—to operate our publishing company in line with the ideas in our books. At the core of our approach is stewardship, which we define as a deep sense of responsibility to administer the company for the benefit of all of our "stakeholder" groups: authors, customers, employees, investors, service providers, and the communities and environment around us.

We are grateful to the thousands of readers, authors, and other friends of the company who consider themselves to be part of the "BK Community." We hope that you, too, will join us in our mission.

A BK Business Book

This book is part of our BK Business series. BK Business titles pioneer new and progressive leadership and management practices in all types of public, private, and nonprofit organizations. They promote socially responsible approaches to business, innovative organizational change methods, and more humane and effective organizations.

Berrett–Koehler
Publishers

A community dedicated to creating
a world that works for all

Dear Reader,

Thank you for picking up this book and joining our worldwide community of Berrett-Koehler readers. We share ideas that bring positive change into people's lives, organizations, and society.

To welcome you, we'd like to offer you a free e-book. You can pick from among twelve of our bestselling books by entering the promotional code **BKP92E** here: http://www.bkconnection.com/welcome.

When you claim your free e-book, we'll also send you a copy of our e-newsletter, the *BK Communiqué*. Although you're free to unsubscribe, there are many benefits to sticking around. In every issue of our newsletter you'll find

- A free e-book
- Tips from famous authors
- Discounts on spotlight titles
- Hilarious insider publishing news
- A chance to win a prize for answering a riddle

Best of all, our readers tell us, "Your newsletter is the only one I actually read." So claim your gift today, and please stay in touch!

Sincerely,

Charlotte Ashlock
Steward of the BK Website

Questions? Comments? Contact me at bkcommunity@bkpub.com.

SFI Certified Sourcing
www.sfiprogram.org
SFI-00453

Certified

B

Corporation
bcorporation.net